A Monk's Alphabet

A MONK'S ALPHABET

*Moments of Stillness
in a Turning World*

JEREMY DRISCOLL, O.S.B.

NEW SEEDS
Boston
2006

NEW SEEDS BOOKS
An imprint of Shambhala Publications, Inc.
Horticultural Hall
300 Massachusetts Avenue
Boston, Massachusetts 02115
www.newseedsbooks.com

9 8 7 6 5 4 3 2 1

First Edition
Printed in the United States of America

Designed by Lora Zorian

♾ This edition is printed on acid-free paper that meets the
American National Standards Institute z39.48 Standard.
Distributed in the United States by Random House, Inc.,
and in Canada by Random House of Canada Ltd

LIBRARY OF CONGRESS CATALOGING-IN-PUBLICATION DATA

Driscoll, Jeremy, 1951–
A monk's alphabet: moments of sillness in a turning world/
Jeremy Driscoll.
p. cm.
Originally published: London: Darton, Longman & Todd, 2005.
ISBN-13: 978-1-59030-373-3 (alk. paper)
ISBN-10: 1-59030-373-3
1. Christian life—Meditations. 2. Vocabulary. I. Title.
BV4501.3.D75 2006
242'.6942—dc22
2006000685

For Paul Murray, O.P.
who helped so much with this alphabet
and who helps so much in general

A Monk's Alphabet

Introduction

A MONK'S DAY IS VERY REGULAR. Prayer always at the same time and structured in the same way. Reading and work at the appointed intervals. Meals at the customary hour and always taken at the assigned place in the refectory. A predictable diet. Always to bed at this hour, always rising from sleep at that hour. The architectural arrangement of the monastery underlines the regularity of these monastic practices. Long corridors uniformly marked by doors to the brethren's cells and to the rooms of common living. It goes on the same one day after another, week after week, for years and years. I have been living in my monastery since 1973. Not much has changed in the way I pass my days.

This terrifying regularity is not meant to drive a person mad, though it has been known to do so. It is not even meant primarily as a form of asceticism, though it does require a certain sense of discipline. It is not a repudiation of variety as the spice of life, though at first it appears flavorless. Rather, it is designed to set the monk free on a different level of his being, and generally it accomplishes just that. Once used to the exterior routine, the monk is free to live much more readily attuned to an interior life, to a realm in which the life of the mind and the spirit holds sway. Only this can make monastic life interesting. However boring or exotic its exterior forms may appear at first glance to those who do not practice them, the exotic dimension quickly disappears for those who carry them out day after day. And yet even these dimensions retain a kind of aura for practitioner and observer alike precisely because they are the concrete forms through which one passes back and forth from one level of life to the other.

So, monastic life arranges the exterior dimensions of human existence in such a way that its interior dimensions can come more immediately to the fore. This is accomplished by establishing a thoroughgoing regularity to the exterior shape of each day. But the life of the spirit, the inner life, that emerges is anything but regular, anything but predictable. It may well be too chaotic and lead to a crash. Yet in most cases—guided by the wisdom embodied in a vast tradition handed down by monks of former generations—the interior life that unfolds produces a variety that is indeed the spice of life. What people see outwardly of a monk's life might lead them to expect that things would be different, that a monk's inner life would be dull and plain. With this book I want to testify, "Not for me it isn't!" With this book I want to share some of my life, not because there is anything especially interesting about *me,* but because the life of the mind and spirit is interesting. I feel the privilege of being able to live in such a way. And I want to bear witness to it.

This book is not a treatise on monastic life; it does not attempt to explain it. And indeed the very form I have chosen for sharing my thoughts is a kind of anti-treatise. I am employing here a genre of thought with a precedent in both ancient monasticism and ancient philosophy. This genre has been employed for millennia, from the philosopher-emperor Marcus Aurelius to the brilliant monastic theologian Evagrius Ponticus, to a figure who in some ways combines the spirit of both of these, Blaise Pascal. Those lovers of wisdom from long ago, chose, among other ways, to express their thoughts and insights in short, provisional essays varying in length from, say, three lines to several hundred. They were written to provoke thought in an interlocutor, the reader. The reader joins the search. No one has the definitive insight, the complete statement, the total resolution of the mystery. We proceed in fits and starts, bits and pieces. But by going and going on, we get somewhere. We have at least this much satisfaction: We are not sitting still before the mystery of life; we are not paralyzed by it.

What I present here is full of starts and stops. The genre allows for it. It allows thoughts on many different levels to follow one after another in no particularly significant order, the way thoughts usually unfold in our own minds. But when we intentionally employ an exercise that lets our thoughts move in this way, we discover all sorts of unexpected connections between what is, at first glance, a series of disjointed thoughts. The many and varied thoughts come together and begin to sketch certain patterns, not created by ourselves trying to remain in control, but formed from a deeper logic which has slowly revealed itself through the thoughts being allowed to flow freely and to touch unpredictably.

In the tradition there are several possible ways of deciding how to set down such provisionally formulated thoughts; for inevitably there is a start to them all and eventually an end and then all that comes between. If the order is not significant, then how are they to be placed? An alphabet is one way, but another way was to play a number game. Evagrius, the fourth-century monk, was good at this. He would write what were called "centuries," that is, a set of a hundred thoughts. Other monks, during hundreds of years, imitated him in this form. Each thought could stand on its own, but it might also take on a certain nuance in relation to other numbers. For example, a chain of ten might play an every-other-one game of tag, linking parts of one thought to another in this way, waiting for the reader to discover the tie. Or a special clue might be tucked away at the beginning, middle, and end of a chain. But no matter what the scheme, the main point is that there is no scheme. Each thought must first stand on its own and, with meditation, be allowed to work its own effect.

I set down my thoughts here in an alphabetical order, having given each one a title of a single word or two. This is a radical version of the genre, for it means to indicate that there is no order at all in which these thoughts need to be read. This book can be used like a dictionary. That is, although you can do so, you don't usually start at the beginning and go through to the end, as must be done in a treatise, following a complicated and carefully developed argument. In a dictionary (and also here) you can read any entry in any order. But if eventually all the entries are read, a language is learned. I want *A Monk's Alphabet* to work like this. I invite my interlocutor to start anywhere and go anywhere, to think with me about all sorts of things that come to mind from a way of life—the monastic life—that promotes the life of mind and spirit. Like a dictionary, so with thoughts offered in alphabetical order: it may be enough to read just one entry. Or, again, like with a dictionary, consulting one entry can lead to another, either just because it happens to be on the same page or because it has brought something else to mind.

Before I begin, I must also confess to something. Although the theme of the unvarying routine of the monastic life has deeply marked my own life during more than three decades, I have also lived through a series of circumstances that contradict in part this supposed exterior monotony. My monastery is in Oregon, in a relatively remote rural scene. It was there that I settled down into the monastic way. But during many years I have also been assigned to study and teach in Rome at a school where Benedictine monks do just that. In the center of a city, in this case Rome, the regular routine of the rural monastery is able to come less to the fore. For more than ten years now I have gone back and forth: half the year in the country, half the year in the city. Ah well, there is ample monastic precedent also for this. For me personally this has been tremendously enriching. From the peace of my rural scene I am thrust into the heart of the city. From the edge of America I am cast into a center of Europe. But wherever I am, I always feel myself guided and provoked by the monastic traditions I live. I am a monk wherever I am.

But if I am a monk, that means also that I am just a man, connected with all other men and women in my time . . . and in other times. I am searching, like we all do. I struggle to believe, like we all do. Life is lovely, life is hard—this is true for me like it is for us all. That is why I think to share my alphabet. Not because monks are different and so worth a visit to see them in a zoo, but because my monastic life has given me the space to think about things that we all care about and all have to face. Life poses huge questions. Terrible questions, glorious questions. We must face them. Avoiding them makes us dangerous and makes the world go crazy.

What is offered here is provisional. There is nothing normative in what is provisional. In the midst of my going on, I turn at any random moment to any random person who might be interested in joining the search. I turn and say, "Oh, think about this."

List of entries

Mass
Material
Message
Midlife
Mistakes
Monastic
Moose
Mosquitoes
Music
Muzzle
Nature
Ninety-three
Nothingness
Nowosielski
Offering
O'Keeffe
Old
Opening
Opportunity
Orchard
Oyster
Pacific Ocean
Pain
Paradise
Paris
Peninsula
Photo
Pimple
Poet
Poland
Prayer
Priest
Principle
Processions
Prose
Psalms
Qualifications

Quest
Questions
Raïssa
Record
Relativity
Relief
Restless
Resurrection
Risks
Roar
Saints
Shooting Star
Slain
Slave
Smugness
Soul
Spiritual
    Direction
Spiritual Warfare
Stability
Stage
Streets
Struggling with
    Prayer
Style
Surprise
Survival
Suspicion
Swinging
Teaching
Tears
Telephone
Tentative
Testaccio
Thread
Three
Time

Time 2
Traces
Transience
Tremendous
Unbearable Sizes
Undone
Unique
United
Unknowing
Unused
Variations
Vocation
Voices
Wager
Walking
Washington, D.C.
We
Weather
White
Words
World
Writing
X-ray of a Cherry
Yawning
You
Young
Zacchaeus
Zerr

AIRPLANE. The winter night is cold and clear. I finish singing compline with my monastic community and step out into the garden where, far from city lights, I look up to the sky and see the million stars. Verses from the psalms still move in me. "He who dwells in the shelter of the Most High . . ." (Ps. 91); " . . . the Lord who made heaven and earth" (Ps. 134); "I will lie down in peace . . ." (Ps. 4). In the stars I see moving fast among them a jet plane and think with affection of its cargo of passengers. I am able to imagine from my own flying how different the same moment is for them, different from my quiet garden. They speed along somewhere, probably a little cramped and uncomfortable; and yet for all that, what they are doing is amazing. They travel at great speed to a desired faraway destination. And given the circumstances, there is relative comfort. The terrible cold is shut out, as well as the night. They can listen to music, watch a movie, drink wines from another continent, do remarkable calculations and other work on their computers.

As a Benedictine monk I live a tradition that is 1,500 years old, but I am not living in another time different from my own. This is my century too. I travel in planes, see the movies, use a computer. It makes me think about how I think. The monastic environment, in fact, offers unique advantages for thinking in a particular way. This environment and these advantages are certainly linked to a tradition, indeed to a very old one. And yet at the same time the one thinking—in this case, me—is also a product of and a player in his own times. That is, he is involved in the kind of world of which jet travel may serve as an emblem. So like any other person living in our times, the monk is potentially a partner and player in a cultural dialogue. He is not disqualified by the ancient traditions to which he adheres. In this fact, among other things, we have in monastic life a clear example of how any tradition works. Traditions are not lived for their own sake. They are valued and lived when they are thought to contain a wisdom still useful for our present and future. I am willing to live according to the 1,500-year-old *Rule of St. Benedict* because I believe it contains a wisdom useful not only for me but for my companions, my race, with whom I live this present period of human history.

ANNIVERSARY. If we name a month and the number of a particular day of the month, we are naming a certain position of the earth in relation to the sun, a position the planet held 365 days previous and will hold again that many days hence. I find this marvelous. I am grateful we have language for this fact and can name it, even if it occurred countless times before ever there was a human species around to speak it. Anniversaries are not purely an arbitrary human construct; there is a real cosmic logic to such remembering. What was this place a year ago today when the sun and the earth were placed just so in relation to each other? What was it at this hour and the next hour, with this light and the next light? What was it a thousand years ago or a hundred thousand? Today is a day that has much about it that has been like this before, and that is much of its intrigue and beauty. Still, there has never been this particular day, this March 21 of this particular set of 365 of them. The uniqueness is likewise wonderful. Today is the anniversary of many, many things—things unknown to us but whose memory is held and cosmically awakened by this particular tilt and slant of earth toward sun as it is just now, today. And what happens today will have its first anniversary a year from now. No one need know it; no one need remember it. It is enough that something happen and that the earth and sun hold its memory in their firm and constant hands.

ANSELMO. When I think of the many kinds of pain and tragedy that people are suffering and that we hear about every day—wars, random violence, floods, earthquakes, painful deaths from diseases, accidents—and when I think of lives interrupted and cut short and then the pain for those who loved them and are left behind, I am struck by how, comparatively speaking, such pain has not approached especially near to me, even if it seems I feel rather deeply the pain in others that I hear about. Then parallel to this is the beauty that I see and hear about: wonderful things and wonderful people in the world; day after day, glorious stories.

Perhaps the view from my room here in Rome, at the monastery of Sant' Anselmo, is an emblem of all this. For nearly three thousand years we know of people living on this same space of land. So much sorrow, so much death has seeped into the ground on which my monastery now stands. And yet so much beauty as well and the ever renewing springtime with its cleansing rains and its warming sun. Right now, in the evening twilight, I am looking out on houses where great happiness and great sorrow are unfolding. For the moment, in my personal life, I am between the two; and that too is a position to be lived. I want to live it prayerfully, thoughtfully; that is, without knowing the details, I want to be in communion with whoever it is that is out there, to suffer with them, to enjoy with them. And doing it from here, from this one window, with these people, whoever they are, I want to join myself to the whole history of my race, to the history of my times, and thereby to the history of other times. I want the life of Christ and the mind of Christ to be strong in me so that my quietly being here, even apparently not especially involved, might in fact be a sort of port of entry for Christ into our spaces and our times. Then I will have served a purpose—randomly perhaps, like some accidental death, but a purpose nonetheless.

A SCENT OF THE HILL. My monastery is on a hill. This makes quite a difference. All of us who live on the hill have come up and down it many times; but every ascent of the hill recalls, on a sliding scale between subconscious and conscious, the first time this upward climb was ever made. That first time was filled with a dizzying range of emotions, for a person comes to live on this hill in order to seek God and is inevitably and all at once excited by the adventure, ready for dedication, and afraid that his strength may not match the hope.

To turn the corner at the bottom of the hill and start the ascent is to turn a corner in life. As you climb upward rather steeply and enter quickly into the tall bank of trees, a separation from a life left behind is quickly effected. The trees are splendid, beautiful, tall. They are like a word from God that whispers and waves a message over you: "You are in a new place," they say, "and life will be different here." The climb is a passage, a space that must be come through, in order to reach what you have come for in the first place: the monastic wisdom that points a way toward God.

The actual physical ascent here is an indistinct combination of both steep and gentle. And so also is the way toward God. Although this is not the climb of a rugged mountain or a sheer cliff, it nonetheless requires some effort, but an effort that is paced and ultimately modest. At the top you suddenly come into the open and its beyond: the church, the monastery, the other buildings gathered round the green, and the views in every direction to the valley and to the mountains close and far behind. An inexpressible fullness fills the heart. A place has clearly been established here; something is definitely going on. For the passage I have made, for my ascent, I am invited in; I am bid to share in it. I feel peace, and I want to be a part.

A place and the lives that unfold in a place inevitably interpenetrate, and there is a reciprocal exchange between them such that each composes the other and accompanies the other. Affection grows. Monks love their place, and the place loves its monks. As the years of my searching for God in this place pass, I love the place more and more because progressively its features and details are gathered into my story. This love stirs in me with every ascent or descent of the hill. If I go down the hill, I am on my way elsewhere and I feel the difference as I descend. If my absence is to be a long one, the emotion of leaving what I love is more sharply borne. On returning from afar, however far, it is in the start of the ascent that I know I am returned home. In the short time it takes to mount upward to the top, all the complicated emotions of what it means to live in this place flash through me and resolve themselves in the climb.

BAGHDAD. On the day the war began, I lay down on the floor, flat on my back, to pray. I stared at the ceiling as if looking for heaven, but I could not even get past that ceiling. Still, it seemed God was somehow present to me. Then slowly I felt a force coming into my body, a terrible force. Suffering from people suffering was pouring into me: the frightened people in Baghdad and the other cities, especially the children, the soldiers on both sides fighting and dying, prisoners being tortured, people flagging for want of food and water. As all this came into me more and more, I felt a terrible imbalance in my body. Anguish, restlessness, near despair, a sense of being cut off from God's love, a sense of the whole human race abandoned by him. From time to time I would think that this is perhaps some sharing in Christ's sufferings, his agony. I suppose I know enough theology to have considered that as a possibility. And although such an understanding is an important guide, it really cannot help much inside the experience itself. Otherwise, how much of a sharing would it be? But at least I know from Christ's example how to pray, and I have at least the theoretical hope that it will turn out as resurrection, a hope that perhaps he was closed off from in the midst of his own agony. In any case, imitating his example, I do not cease to cry out "Father!" In fact, I use all of the seven last words of Jesus on the cross to guide my prayer now.

In daily living it seems like it would be a good contribution to be beside others with a greater graciousness and kindness. I try this, but the whole world seems on edge, myself included. All the more reason, though, to keep on trying. I want to thank God for every day of life and live life's joys in humility. But also here I falter. I have a sense of not deserving to live so well while others are suffering so terribly. Yet this is in God's hands, not mine. If today, while war rages elsewhere, he gives me a peaceful day, food to eat, and good people all around me, then I want to thank him in all humility and cherish his gifts. I remember the example of Czeslaw Milosz, who continued to write lyric poetry during the worst days of World War II.

I feel in me a terrible something that I sense as vibrating through the whole world, as gripping billions of human hearts; namely, a sense that we are cut off from God and are left to our own worst instincts. But for the Christian such a thought must be considered a lie, the very conclusion desired by the Evil One who incites us to these wars. So, I am trying to battle against that thought. If the content of Christian faith and hope can vibrate in me, then maybe it can spread to the countless others who are also under the terrifying spell. Doing good—this will be my resistance to what the war has unleashed.

BEETHOVEN. When I was nineteen, I had a summer job as a cowboy in New Mexico. I went with three friends, none of whom, like me, knew much about serious riding and work with cattle, but we went to learn, ready for the adventure. We were trained in our new skills by riding alongside real cowboys, both boys and men who had been raised in that land and in that work. Riding home at the end of the day, there often would be long hours of banter. We were amused by the real cowboys, and they were amused by us. The banter would often include the rubric of insulting the horse that the other was riding that day. You were expected to defend your own horse and trash the others.

Some new horses had recently been added to our

herd and were without names. We saw that these horses would eventually be dubbed according to what they revealed of themselves after several days of riding. And so our horses had names like Dime (short for Diamond), Dent (caught in barbed wire and so putting a dent in his flank), Flash (who was fast), and other such names, usually of one syllable. One of our new horses was an impressive bay, with beautiful proportions of the black markings on brown that characterize this coloring. My three friends and I took to calling him Beethoven—to honor his beauty, to suggest that there was strong music in his gait. The real cowboys heard with curiosity our three-syllable name for the splendid steed, and in the banter coming home one late afternoon, Beethoven's rider (clearly unaware of the great musician of the same name) asked me, "Why you calling my bay Beethoven?" The Muse of Banter entered me in a flash, and I thought in that moment, sweetly inspired, to say, "Because a toven is a no-good horse and you're riding a bay, so it's a bay-toven." He didn't know the word *toven,* and fair enough, for, as I say, it had only just then been invented. But he immediately responded, "Well, it's a bay, but it ain't no toven."

For the rest of the summer *toven* was a word of our banter vocabulary. We all came to use it in the varying contexts in which there was reason to criticize a horse. I've often wondered if the word might still be in use in that region. I imagine some future entry in a dictionary: *toven,* a flawed horse; regional only, Southwest USA; origin unknown.

BENEDICT. As a Benedictine monk, I am naturally inspired by the figure of St. Benedict, whose wise document, which we call *The Holy Rule,* is the basis of our way of life. He was born in Norcia in Umbria in 480, lived for a while as a student in Rome, left the city disillusioned, and became a hermit monk in Subiaco. After fame of his holiness and wisdom spread, he was pressured into founding what became a great monastery, Montecassino. It was there that he wrote *The Holy Rule,* which exercised enormous influence throughout the subsequent history of Europe. He was dead by the year 550.

All that we know of his life comes to us from St. Gregory the Great, who was himself a monk before he was pope from 590 to 604. On the cusp of the sixth and seventh centuries, the bishop of Rome lived in a world that is not without parallels to our own. The Roman Empire was crumbling all around him, the culture that had carried the best of pagan and Christian insight was vanishing, and the invasion of barbarians raised the question of whether it would be any longer possible to live the Christian life in-depth. One of the ways in which Gregory attempted to give light and hope in such a situation was by recounting the life of St. Benedict. One of the stories of that life has been especially formative for me. I use it as an image of how I want to work and what I want to think about as a monk and theologian.

The scene that Gregory describes begins with St. Benedict seated quietly at the door of his monastery, absorbed in reading. Suddenly, crashing unexpectedly into the peace of the scene, there comes riding up on a horse a rough-mannered and haughty barbarian, shoving before him a poor peasant, who is bound with ropes. The peasant owes the barbarian money and has claimed that his goods are deposited in the safekeeping of Benedict's monastery. Without any introduction or any attempt at graciousness, the barbarian shouts at Benedict, "Get up! Get up! No tricks, just get me this guy's money, which he says you have." What follows is a quintessential monastic moment. It is, if you will, the monastic contribution to the world, the world being represented here in one of its unhappier aspects by the barbarian. We are told that, in response to the barbarian's rude and abrupt command, St. Benedict calmly raised his eyes from his reading and looked for a moment at the barbarian. Slowly his gaze turned toward the poor peasant, noting how cruelly he was bound. This is an image of monastic reading; this is an image of Christian contemplation. The monk, looking up from the Scripture, fixes his gaze on the suffering of the world. In that moment in which Benedict's eyes fall on the suffering man—it could be called the moment in which the light of Scripture penetrates the darkness of human suffering and injustice—a tremendous wonder is worked. The knots in the ropes that bound the man suddenly unravel, and he stands there completely free. He, of course, was not displeased; and the barbarian was terribly impressed. The latter in fact, threw himself at St. Benedict's feet, asking for his prayers. Benedict effortlessly returned to his reading, ordering several of the monks to prepare some refreshment for the barbarian. As he was about to depart, Benedict simply took the occasion to tell him not to treat others so cruelly.

With wisdom like this—calm and kind, attentive and straightforward, anchored in the Word of God— St. Benedict created the monasticism that was to have such an impact in the history of Christian Europe and eventually in many other parts of the world. It is a wisdom still needed by us today: in the midst of the massive inhumanity we direct toward one another and see all around us, to stay calmly anchored in the Word of God and to let its power set us free.

BETWEEN THE LINES. Of course, God cannot be just another of the things of this world, to be noticed also alongside all the rest. God's very being requires more than that, not *more* in the sense of quantity but in the sense of quality. And so, if God is here at all—and God must be because all the rest is— then it would have to be in the quality of something like "between the lines" of things and persons, of something like the desire that others awaken in us but never satisfy, of something like a hidden radiance that we are longing to see, whose presence we sometimes suspect, but never see.

So then, this is a fine mess: a concrete, marvelous, beautiful world of things and people, and yet no ultimate satisfaction in it, only an increasingly restless heart. I am longing for the divine glory hidden in everything to burst forth and present itself to our vision. How much longer must we wait for this? As the delay continues, our faith and hope naturally weaken. How are we not to look to particular people and things—so exquisite, so beautiful—to satisfy our longing, even when we know quite well that they cannot? All this must be what inspired that poor and simple prayer, "Come, Lord, delay your coming no longer."

BIBLE. Why does a person write? To find a thought. To give form and body to an intuition. To find what it is that makes an idea hold together. Great authors keep repeating themselves. Something profound lies in this. They are working through a few big thoughts and intuitions. These come from the heart; they rise up; and one tries to sound the music in a thousand different ways. It is a thought, a set of thoughts, or one complex thought, that is lived through many years.

The Bible shares in this mystery of writing. It has many human authors, but it is also one big book by one same divine author, who is working out one complex thought. Or it is a whole library of books by this author, employing many literary genres. But what is this writing? It can be pondered from different points of view. They are all placed within a narrative form: "In the beginning . . ."—these are the very first words of the very first page, but that structure holds all the way through to the last pages of Revelation. *Covenant* is perhaps the single most unitary theme of this divine author. Very interesting also, is the idea of intervention, God's great, surprising, unexpected interventions in human history. God *is* the one who intervenes in history from above. In any case, the image of God is continually refined throughout the course of this book, slowly molding historical figures to form one complex figure: a new Moses, a new David with a new covenant—the awaited Messiah. It is overloaded writing. There are many meanings, many interpretations. In a sense, they are all literal meanings because they are part of what the book has come to mean.

The Bible is like a church—centuries old—that has seen restorations in many styles (e.g., Baroque inside Romanesque) and then is restored to a supposed original, which never in fact really existed. This supposed original is the way that hard-core historical-critical exegesis tries to read the Bible sometimes. But all the periods, all the interpretations have a kind of truth—and especially all of them together.

Yet ultimately we are not talking about the Bible until we have faced the strangeness of the Christian Bible and its central message: resurrection. This is something utterly unique, even if we have become too used to hearing it. But it is an extraordinary claim: the survival of each individual historical existence. If this is so, everything is new. History, as we would otherwise conceive it, is over. A new time opens. It is a definitive passage.

BLACK HOLE. We are just a few hours away from evening prayer on Christmas Eve, and with our singing we will begin the feast. The day is crisp, cold, and blue—beautiful. There is a lovely slanted light from the feeble sun. I feel quite empty, and I am not expecting to feel otherwise, yet I hope this might be my learning a new kind of hope, hope that is deeper in and less like joys that are too bluntly material. But I do not know. It may just be a great emptiness.

The visual image is that of having a black hole in the middle of me, in my stomach or in the place where my stomach is meant to be. All around it, the rest of my body and even my person continue to function. I have thoughts, I say and do the right things, I feel the feelings that people feel, I even help people and encourage them. But all of this circles around a darkness in the middle of me.

When I ask myself, "What is it? What does the darkness mean?" I move between two poles as I grope toward an answer. One pole says that this is Evil and all of its awesome power to devour and destroy me, to destroy us all. The other pole says that it is the luminous darkness of the mystery of God. Or to combine the poles in the terms of the Christmas feast: it is God's light come cloaked in the garment of flesh and the garment of sin.

With this hole in the middle of me I will celebrate the liturgy and participate in all the festive gatherings. Lord, show me the way I should go and save me from crumbling. The words of John's prologue describe my hope: "The light shines in the darkness, and the darkness has not overcome it" (John 1:5).

B LACK STARS. Paul Murray's book, *These Black Stars,* arrived in the mail the other day; and I am enjoying reading again on the handsome printed page all the poems I have read before in the manuscript, many of which I had read and discussed with him. As I finished it a first time and read the last poem, called "Beginning," I wondered if I would ever write a poem with such sentiments. I would like to; I am just wondering if it can ever happen for me. He begins,

> Now after a long night
> Of stillness and longing

That is the night in which I still find myself; and being in the midst of it I wonder if I will ever be able to speak of an "after" to such a night. A few lines later he says

> And what I had despaired of so long is here.

I am still despairing, and I see no after.

Ah well—as so many of his poems suggest, if something changes for me, it will not be my own doing but a grace received. I am waiting.

BLUNTLY. To state it bluntly: Jesus Christ puts me in a relationship with God otherwise impossible to me.

BREATHLESS. I'm in Paris, and Ghislain and I saw a splendid French classic film this afternoon, Jean-Luc Godard's *À bout de souffle,* or, in English, *Breathless,* made in 1959, filmed in Paris, on the streets we pass. It seems primitively made by today's standards, but that precisely is its force. It has the feel of Hitchcock from the same period, at least insofar as the camera is so well used, always speaking by its unexpected angles and many overdrawn scenes. You still feel cinema as a genre of art and not merely, as it is so often now, simply a technical wonder. Ghislain says that all of Godard's films treat the theme of our inability to love. *Breathless* is certainly about that. A totally cool gangster is betrayed by a New York girl come to Paris, and he truly loves her in his own way. She experiments (shamefully) with him, and in the end he dies for it. His last words are directed to her: "You're a lousy bitch." Then he reaches up, closes his own eyes, and dies.

B UGS. My room, with its open windows, is filling with ladybugs and potato bugs. I don't mind, though I wish there were not so many. Yet they are quiet and seem clean, unlike the annoying and now sluggish flies, every one of which I would gladly kill. This October afternoon is magnificent. The air is clear and warm. The sun on the valley discloses a miracle of colors: scores of kinds of green in fields and trees, marvelous ranges of browns in other fields and in the changing leaves, yellows and oranges and reds in others of the leaves, even a great patch of black in a nearby field burned yesterday.

Why does this vision not calm me and give me peace? I think because it is all passing and even now, for the most part, is unseen. And even if seen, so what? What does it mean? What is it all for?

The bugs are coming into my room because they know that soon it will be too cold for them. It won't be long. We needn't wait till winter. The autumn cold will annihilate them. In here, with me, they will last a little longer. But again, so what? It is no wonder we have constructed ways of living that make us insensitive to all that is around us, including one another. Who can absorb this much mystery? Who can bear its burden? A thousand years ago, ten thousand years ago, there would have been a bright afternoon like today's in this season of the year. Bugs swarming, panicked at the coming cold. What were those days then? What is this day now?

BURGUNDY. Splendid countryside, holding very still under the hot sun. On the bus I was looking at the land, admiring it and thinking about Christ. Did I feel his presence? Perhaps. Something filled me briefly between my thoughts and the vision of the land. Perhaps it was he. In any case, it was something very big, elusive, wide like the land, textured like the land, peaceful like my thoughts. I wanted to talk to him directly, to say things to him and interiorly to be sure of his response. But there was none of that. Yet perhaps all that was Christ, ever so much bigger than my small what-I-have-to-say-to-him and what I wish he would say back.

CHILDHOOD. This morning at vigils (the feast of the Holy Innocents, December 28) we read a homily from John Henry Newman where he was speaking about the nature of childhood innocence and the process whereby we lose it. At one point he spoke of "what we once were" (i.e., children) as an intimation of what God will make us in the kingdom of heaven.

This is an amazing thought, bigger than what it seems on first impact. I am accustomed to think of time passing as time in which I should be growing toward what I will be, and there is some clear sense in which this is true. But Newman gets at another level of the question here. His suggestion helps me to intuit, to detect in me, a someone I once already was as a part of what I am becoming. Even if I never was that someone completely, I have already touched it, already been that. It is—I catch a glimpse in flashes—being that person that God would have intended me to be before the fall, his idea of me before the history of sin begins to kick in and have its actual effects on my life.

I think of Joe T. and Keenan E., two seven-year-old boys, so excited and pure as I helped them prepare for their first communion. I was standing at the altar with them and explaining different things about the Mass, telling them deep things boldly that adults would have understood with difficulty. Suddenly Joe shuddered and exclaimed, "How do you know these things?" Then I think of John N., sixteen, who used to have that same innocence but is now losing it. He recently told me, sullen and accepting, "It used to be that God was always there, that I felt his presence always. Then one day it all went away." That is what often happens. But what is that? Why?

CITY AND COUNTRY. Today, in the monastic choir, singing along in one of the psalms about Jerusalem being restored, there flashed through my mind a strong visual image of the actual city as it is today. With Father Konrad singing next to me in choir, who loves Jerusalem so much and lived there for a number of years, I thought what a privilege it is to live today in some great city—Jerusalem, Rome, Barcelona, New York, San Francisco—that has exerted and continues to exert some strong influence on history and culture. To live in such a city, even as just one of millions, is to be a part of something grand.

Then I wondered if I am living anything less grand out here in the country where I am. And I think not. Yet there is probably no need to contrast country with city and to imagine one as better than the other. Today I am letting the life of the city—how glorious it is to be a part of it—be a guide for me in discovering something important, something historical and cultural, about being a citizen of a particular piece of country. It is perhaps less obvious, but there is a grandeur waiting to be discovered in my living in this portion of the valley in this particular season of the year, a grandeur comparable in scope and in importance to the grandeur of being a part of Jerusalem or Rome or one of the other greats. Jerusalem can be a guide—indeed, God so intended it—to living in any city on earth and in any piece of country. I have sung of this often (out here in the country) in another psalm: "Of Zion they shall say, 'One and all were born in her.' People shall be enrolled saying, 'This one was born in her.' All shall sing and dance saying, 'All my origins are in you'" (Ps. 87:5–7).

CLUMSY. All my longing, all my restlessness, my worry, my sense of failure—perhaps all this is just my clumsiness at finding myself in contact with the divine and eternal realities in which I am immersed. I mean God. I am immersed in God through the finite forms he has created and placed among us as means for touching his infinite form. Of course, one is all mixed up at first.

CONNECTIONS. Passing full and near perfect days in an Oregon summer has the strange effect of etching more clearly in my memory and mind certain scenes from Europe. I am in the valley, not even at the coast, but somehow now I have a splendid set of visual memories of walks along the shore of the Adriatic in a festive explosion of a unique quality of light, and then I remember drives from there in the country hills with the setting sun, the *paesaggio*

beyond. Or I am thinking of scenes of Barcelona, its long and noble streets, its abundance of trees, cooling us in the summer heat and the late nights. Or the neighborhood of Prati in Rome on a hot summer evening on my way to Louis and Kate's house. There is a place in the orchard here that makes me think of Poland and not of an orchard in Poland but of a street in Kraków. I don't get the connection, but in the orchard I think this street. I also remember terraced banks of olive trees outside of Florence many years ago at the house of Donatella, my Italian teacher. Or Mount Saint Victoire in Provence during a summer there and pictures by Cézanne. One world. My one life. Mysterious waiting-to-be-understood connections.

CONTEMPORARIES. We think of our families and relatives. We think of our nation or race. We regard the geographical unit in which we live. We identify with others of our same faith. In all these ways we find the bonds that establish us in relation to others. Not everyone is included. We need a set of relations. We cannot be connected evenly to one and all. But there is another kinship that we tend perhaps too much to overlook. I mean the tie with my contemporaries: all the people who are alive now while I am alive, and this across different countries and any culture. Reflecting on this, I find a kinship strangely strong. The thought inspires a tenderness in me for all others who are alive now in this same period of human time in which I too have appeared. It reveals a potential relationship and bond with anyone at all who is alive while I am, from whatever land or whatever culture. No matter the differences in personal cultures or personal stories, there will always be this wonderful possibility of real meeting and real kinship simply in virtue of our being alive at the same time. Everybody else is on a schedule different from mine, but our times overlap. Older people are still alive and can relate to me, their junior. And I am able to meet any of those who got started after me, and we can have real points of contact. The world moves along in this way. The web is immense. My contemporaries, my relatives! We move together for a brief while through the span of life that is given us.

CONTINUITY. There is, of course, a continuity in my life from who I was as a child to the man I now am. There is an explanation for how and why I am who I am. But I have lost the thread. I forget how I got here. What would happen if I should remember, should recover the thread?

CREATION. The whole created world is already God's open and gracious communication of himself. One needn't go elsewhere or leave it behind in order to meet him. Our (inevitable) encounter with created realities is already our encounter with God. If after that God wishes also to communicate even more of himself somehow, then, of course, it is his choice as to how. In fact, what we see in Jesus is that God, using his creation as a foundation through which he continues to communicate, also does even more. The becoming flesh of the Eternal Word is the model and pattern of his continually unfolding choice: God himself immediately present in his mediating creation. Recapitulating everything in heaven and on earth in Christ. Man gives voice to voiceless creation, but the Incarnate Word gives voice to voiceless man.

CROSS. I was praying before the painted cross in the abbot primate's chapel. It is hundreds of years old, going back to the thirteenth or fourteenth century. It is beautiful. The dead body of Christ is so giving, filled with light, and surrounded by angels. I thought of it hanging somewhere, looking like that, every day during all those centuries. I thought of all the events of history that have unfolded. And no matter how diverse the materials of history and the continents on which all the various things have happened, this cross was hanging somewhere, absorbing the events and judging them all, suited to every situation. It is art's way of saying what the sacraments also accomplish in their own way: the hour of Jesus' dying is an hour which does not pass away, which draws all things to itself.

CROWDS. I was praying after compline one evening before the Blessed Sacrament and became aware, after about ten minutes, of Father Martin (age ninety-two) rising, cautiously genuflecting, and then advancing slowly and quietly down the hall into the cloister of the monastery. It occurred to me that heaven for him—and hopefully also for me—will not be altogether different from that moment: adoration, silence, a moving along forward into a great blank of something both familiar and unknown, and he and I being together but focusing on the Lord. What was especially new for me in this insight was noticing that in my thinking about heaven I usually tend to have a sense—only half explicit, but solidly there—of crowds, crowds of angels and saints in a great communion of adoration. But in this moment there was such silence and simplicity and intimacy in my being with the Lord, and I could sense that kind of a moment extending itself right on into heaven with people like Father Martin walking along the side of my consciousness, only thousands more like him. And countless numbers of angels everywhere, and yet still my intimacy with the Lord, or my great emptiness in his presence, or whatever it is.

CRUELTY. The cruelty of the world—how old was I when it first began to dawn on me?

CRUMBLING. The world seems more and more to be crumbling. More people are awaking to the strange mood. Folks are really acting crazy, and there is a vicious spirit abroad in the land. I am feeling so tired of it; and as I try to pray in response, I feel my own weakness and I struggle to hope. For it seems my world of faith and the Church are crumbling too. And my monastery. And the things I do.

From one angle I look at all this with relative dispassion and think through several possible constructs for understanding it. The best-case scenario for my coming to grips with the despair that threatens to over-whelm me personally is that this is simply an invitation to deeper faith and hope. If my way is particularly dark and yet I still push through, then this could be useful to others, a sort of pioneering effort through the new territory of this strange moment in the history of the world. Worst case scenario is that the wickedness in us all has been somehow unleashed, and the world will finish first in a savage bloodbath and finally in a dirty nuclear holocaust.

With the same dispassion and clarity—it seems a clarity to me, though it may not be—I try to pray. My prayer is either just what is called for or a huge nothing which at least causes no harm. I shall try to persevere in prayer despite the severe temptation to think that it is nothing, that no one is listening. I see no way out of this dilemma because prayer with no one listening may be some mysterious being conformed to the cross of Christ, who, after all, cried out, "My God, My God, why have you forsaken me?" Or it may simply be no one listening. The safest bet is to continue in hope.

It seems impossible to me to imagine or conceive anything greater than the content and claims of Christian faith—obviously not these as poorly represented but as they really are. These do not seem human in their origin. They are so refined; they are more than human; they are divine. Is their greatness an argument for their truth? If so, why does it not persuade all or even at least more? *Living* the Christian life is the only argument, the only way forward. I am trying to live from the old truths in this new and changed time.

DENSITY. As I sit quietly in this country place, I think of the adventure of those two months. It was primarily a mental adventure, but I know it to be real by the not inconsiderable concrete experience of going to the places that were a part of it: to Paris, to Kraków, to Auschwitz, up the stairs to Milosz's apartment, down the streets with Maciej and Ghislain. I feel a large store of something new within me as a result of having so traveled in mind and body, but I am hard-pressed to say what it is. Yet I want badly to know. There was such density to those days. I need to understand them. I want to do something or make something as a response. But what? And must I?

DESIGN. There is a room in a house on the Via San Domenico in Rome where I am some-times able to go and write. Like every part of this house, this room has its special genius, a neatly and precisely defined space with its own mood. Where I work it is uncluttered and filled with a wonderful light that spills in through the tall window on my left. All the details of the house are Danilo Parisio's designs, and every bit of it is handsome and fine. The proportions of everything—they are so learned, clearly fitted by one who knows what he is doing.

Out of this window, as I turn to rest my eyes and my mind from the work of composing at the computer, I can practice what I read the other day in Milosz's poem called "This Only." He spoke of wanting "only one most precious thing: to see, purely and simply . . ."

What makes the garden beyond the window such a joy to see from here is the way in which the window frames and holds what I see. It seems an odd thing to utter enthusiastic exclamations about, but I want to keep crying out in appreciation, saying, "The proportions! The proportions!"

The mimosa tree, whose trunk is well beyond my sight, sends its bright yellow branches over for display directly before the window. Whether I turn to it directly or not, its yellow comes silently into my white room; and all through my day of writing, consciously as I turn to look, subconsciously as I turn back again to write, I am tinged within and without by the first colors of the spring. I am in a great house where, comfortable and warm, I work with all that is outside close in around me.

Now the tree's branches are still, and the light is

waning. During the course of the day, the branches, heavy with their bloom and with the frequent rains, would bounce slowly up and down under the impulse of the soft and occasional winds. I would catch the movement out the corner of my eye and turn toward it as if in answer to a summons. What a worthy distraction! Or was my work the distraction? In any case, the pleasure and beauty of the scene was enhanced by my seeing it through the noble proportions of the window's frame. The frame, utterly still and firm. Strong tall white lines with their comparatively narrow cross-width—and in the open space beyond, the bouncing heavy-laden branches in their varied movements. Alive, alive, alive—the whole world is alive and moving. Not just me and the tree, but also the house and the room and the window. Also the clouds and the sky behind and above the tree, the roof and the dull red tiles that I espy through the live thicket beyond. We are all alive together and bound into varying constellations by the live numbers of the proportions through which we see and touch each thing and the next.

DEVIL. Nicolas Steinhardt was carted off to prison in Romania in the worst period of the Communist regime. His crime: intelligence, culture, class. In prison he became a Christian and after his release, a monk. He has written a remarkable book, full of little and large wisdoms, whose English title would be *Diary of Happiness*. He says there that the evils of the twentieth century are patently clear to anyone at all, and so it is plainly demonstrated that the devil exists and is near. Consequently, he continues, these times are the most prepared to become Christian. Such claims earn at best a kindly smirk and would be considered naïve in comfortable American suburbs and academia. But in the mind of a Central European who has lived through a good part of the twentieth century, it is the scoffers who seem naïve. What should be patently clear to anyone at all is not clear to them.

DIGNITY. There is a sense in which (also and always) we see ourselves from the outside and so make a certain impression on ourselves. For this reason it is very important always to conduct oneself with dignity and grace, even (and perhaps especially) when alone. It is when we are alone that we probably make the strongest impression on ourselves. If I pull out dignity and grace only when I am with others, well how authentic or full can it be? I am always making an impression on myself, and so I ought to be careful. I am always making an impression on myself, and this is the same impression I should make on others.

DIRECTIONS. I am willing to be directed by my faith, and so I pause to get my directions straight again. The Bible teaches me that I am made in the image of God (Gen. 1:27), and so why not look to that of which I am image to understand also myself? Concretely, this means I can look at Jesus, "the image of the invisible God" (Col. 1:15) and so come to understand myself. And the converse is true: If I do not look at him, I do not know myself.

DYING. I have this intuition about my death and how it will occur—not its circumstances but rather the framework in which it will unfold. It will be my entering into that bright darkness of Jesus' own dying in which he experienced an abandonment by the Father and yet from its depths expressed his own abandonment into the hands of the Father, calling out his name "Father" to the very last. So would I die; and I pray, "Jesus, grant me this grace."

It seems to me that perhaps every death moves in varying proportions between these two poles, the sense of abandonment and the trustful invocation; and for myself, I do not know in which direction I shall be inclined more to lean. In one sense I feel strongly the desire to let my death be a joyful offering, "Father, into your hands I commend my spirit . . . ." And yet when the time comes, it is difficult to know how it will be. Christ may ask of me some deep sharing in his own sense of being abandoned; and if he does, I must count it a privilege. My heart has been practicing, forced to it by circumstances of life, by lesser versions of darkness. But even if I am called to a death like his, I will have one thing that I know Jesus did not. I will have him with me, and I will have the knowledge of resurrection, accomplished and already tasted, as my hope and guide.

I would like to think that in my dying I could be a good example to others, even a beautiful icon of the Lord himself, as Abbot Bonaventure was to all of us when he died. And yet I may become frightened, scared, unsure, invited so deeply into the mystery of abandonment that my death would be a fearful agony. But I hope that no matter what, it could be said by any who might see me die, altering the words in St. Mark's account just slightly, "Seeing that he *thus* breathed his last, they said, 'Truly Jesus is the Son of God'" (Mark 15:39). May my *thus* be like Jesus' *thus*.

E FFORT. Only by suffering and working does someone realize the promise of his life and achieve results never entirely merited.

EGG. We hardly think of it when we do it, but to do it without breaking it a knowledge is required that is acquired. I mean picking up an egg with the right force. Too much and it would break all gooey in my hand. Too little and I drop it. But surely many other things are like this, and the egg is its image. The egg as image of moderation! I need to learn this. Moderation is an acquired knowledge of not too much and not too little, and its application changes according to circumstances. Not to break the egg and not to let it drop—the goal of my life.

ELIJAH. Elijah retraces the steps of Moses but in reverse. Elijah leaves the promised land and returns to the desert, and now God appears, not as he did to Moses in fire, storm, and earthquake, but instead in the tiny whispering sound of a gentle wind, the Spirit.

ENDING. The day is ending in great beauty, and I see again the magnificence of God's plan. A strong wind blew the whole day, very cold again. The air is pure and clean as God intended for our breathing. My vision can reach long while the sun sets. The moon, nearly full, is already high and poised to take over the night. The Alban Hills line up like a dance, and again I admire their broad rhythms. I can see the statues atop the church of the Lateran. Christ and his apostles, their backs to me, turn pink in the last light; and I take it as a greeting from them, even if I do not discern a specific message. Clouds that have never been, being only today's clouds, raced through the sky all day. With what grace they still fly by in day's last light!

ENGELBERG. We three monks had slept well on the night train between Rome and Lucerne and did not awaken until it had grown solidly light and we were well into Switzerland. We pulled the shades of the window open and were presented with a wondrous winter morning: snow falling lightly on several feet already accumulated but visibility good enough to see half way across the frozen lake that the train was rounding. The train would stop in Lucerne before we were really fully awake.

In Lucerne we board a little train specially equipped for the steep climb to the village and monastery of Engelberg, some thirty miles distant, some two thousand feet higher. (Engelberg had founded my monastery in America, called Mount Angel, in 1881. Mount Angel is the English equivalent of the German Engelberg.) The day was clearing as we climbed, but the already fallen snow was growing deeper and deeper. The mountains all round grew steeper and more numerous. The train penetrated a deep forest of fir; all the branches hung downward, heavy-laden with snow. I knew the trip was to take about an hour. After about forty-five minutes the train stopped a moment in the thick forest and somehow kicked into another gear. My anticipation mounted as we did. The climb grew sharper than I thought trains could climb. We were moving very slowly. Everyone on the train grew silent, it seemed, from joy and wonder. At the top we came level into a wide valley laid out at the base of many mountains roughly circling it. These were powerful mountains, many peaks rising some six and seven thousand feet above the valley floor. The sky was now clear and blue but laced with light clouds that looked like snow blowing from off top the distant summits. We entered the village, but I could not see the monastery. I was looking all around for clues, expectant and gladly impatient. We were directed down a street, then another, winding among shops of various kinds. At last we swung round and saw the huge monastery at the end of the town, its onion-domed tower, its church, the cloister—all of it framed by the mountain whose shape the facade of the church clearly echoed.

This was my mother cloister. These were my roots. This was the monastery that founded mine. What would I find here? The large oak door swung open to receive us. The guest master, who knew monks from the daughter house were arriving, was waiting for us with a warm embrace and summoned us to hot coffee with whipped cream. We passed a corridor with windows onto an interior court with many views toward the mountains. I saw a date etched into the stone floor of the corridor: 1740. We entered a sweetly heated room, paneled with wood, a wooden floor, portraits of fifty-seven abbots, dating from 1120, hanging all around. A place visually so different from Mount Angel but a place where I immediately felt all that I feel at Mount Angel: the spirit of a place, the spirit of the Benedictine way, the spirit of Mount Angel's and Engelberg's way, a way refined and nuanced by fifty-seven abbots since 1120. In that moment, there in Switzerland, I became more Mount Angel. I was very glad and profoundly grateful. The privilege of my vocation!

EQUINOX. A couple of years ago on the autumn equinox, I took careful note of the precise time when the sun broke over the mountains that stand on the eastern edge of my valley. It occurred to me that, subtracting an hour for daylight saving time, the time would tell me the relation to "true time" in this place. That is, it can't literally be the same time across the hundreds of miles in a time zone. That's only a convention and an arrangement to lend some unity to a region. Since my place is more or less along the forty-fifth parallel, I reasoned equinox should mean sunrise at six and sunset at six. Well, the sun came up at just seven minutes after the hour, seven minutes after seven, which really was seven minutes after six. That's wonderful. We are only seven minutes off true time here. It was a different true time in north Idaho, where I grew up, more than three hundred miles to the east and yet in the same time zone. "Seven Minutes Off"—perhaps a good title for a poem.

ESCHATOLOGY. The redemption, our being "saved," is eschatological. That is to say, it is more *there* than *here*, more in the *future* than in the *present*. Christ is risen and has ascended into the future he has prepared for us. He is coming again from there, but he is not yet returned. Still, there are signs in the present that come from this future. I mistake them if I expect from them any more than some indication. For example, the liturgy—whether in its beauty and splendor or in its humble and meager shape—is a sign, but only a sign. I taste my future and celebrate it but return to my present. People I love and lovely people are likewise a sign. But we also disappoint one another and hope wrongly for too much from one another. Still, real love lasts and carries us through to the future, even beyond death.

EVERYBODY. Sometimes and often—like today again, for example—I experience my inner life as being so filled with riches, with beautiful gifts from beyond me, that I think it cannot possibly be given for me alone but must somehow belong to everybody. The problem is that I receive it as so particularly mine that I have no sense of how possibly to transfer it from myself to others. And is it not perhaps simply some version of vanity or self-centeredness to imagine that what is particularly mine has a relevance for everybody?

What is the richness and beauty I am speaking of? Mostly about prayer or things heard in prayer that also turn into wisdoms useful in daily living. But I should not make a problem of this. I do not know how to make the transfer anyway, so for the moment at least there is nothing to do. And I am not sure anyway that it all does belong to others and should be expressed.

I ask God to make a way clear should he want me

to share it and to make my heart calm should he not. I thank him for his goodness to me. Meanwhile, I am silent before his great mystery. "My life is hidden now with Christ in God" (Col. 3:3). Perhaps it shall always be. This has been known before to be a Christian's vocation and particularly a monastic vocation: a life of secret riches passing unknown to all but Christ and me in the monastery.

EXCELLENCE. "I kiss my hand to the stars." This line from Gerard Manley Hopkins expresses how I feel about this day. I kiss the day, and I praise the excellence of God. Everything today was a treasure. Released a little somehow from precise religion, I saw all things in a fresh and godly light. Life going on. The inexorable press toward the glory of being, despite all that is squalid about us. A going on in life that has its press and force even in those who have little wisdom and so whose living is shallow. People: the centuries and the present moment combined in their faces. The way they walk, the way they stand, their speaking, a wondrous light in their eyes. And Rome supporting it all. Rome being here, with its colors, its rambling streets, the opening into the squares, flowers in a window, and traffic. Why all this? Whatever is it for?

I sang vespers tonight, half outside of it because I

wasn't especially focused. But the force of its images and music carried me along. How our male voices swelled! What great strength there was in the air that swung the notes upward toward the wooden boat–like beams of the roofs that were the skies. It was a divine something, and I could stand inside of it and out, an uncomprehending man. Whoever God is, God was there and so was I. The smell of incense ran right up my nostrils and quickened my invisible soul. I was weak and strong in that hour: the immensity of God and his excellence blending with my smallness and holding it aloft, holding it somehow to the task, letting me succeed, however improbably, in being there, in being where Life is, where Life manifests itself as un-accountable and quite beautifully there, unpredictable in its myriad nuances, new in every hour and in every minute of the hour.

How shall I stand before all this? How shall I wor-ship? How shall I live? "I kiss my hand to the stars." I kiss the day. I praise the excellence of God.

Rain that threatened all day is finally falling in this night. "Greetings, Rain," I want to say. "So you have come at last." And I want to say this same "you" to everything. You, O Night! You, O quietly moving Clouds! You, screaming and love-making cats! You, O wall beside the road beneath the window behind which I live! You, O Prepositions of my language and all you other parts of speech! I know you well and love you. I have passed the day with you. And: I praise you in your excellence, O God, You who are everywhere.

EXPERIENCING. What I am about to say has been thought through often enough; I am not expressing an original insight. But I would like to live with a little more attention to it, for it is something at which to marvel. When I experience an event, and still more when I recount it, I am massively shaped in the way I experience it by thousands of my memories of previous events. Further, I have developed habits of recounting—first to myself and then to others—that hugely inform the present recounting. So, any present is my past! But there is more: any present is also my future since the future experience will be filtered through the now present event, destined to be past to the coming future. In that sense my future is already here; I am already in part living it.

EXPRESSION. We think that when we see one another, we are seeing primarily the body. But really, it is more the soul than the body that we are seeing. We know how to read especially the face, but indeed the whole body, in its *expression;* and we read it immediately, instinctively. In fact, the very word *expression* implies this: what is in itself invisible achieves visibility in the bodily expression of another. Actually, I see the other's soul before I see the body *qua* body. When another comes toward me, what I first see, what I first detect, is that one's feeling, the inner life, his sense of this encounter with me. Only in seeing this do I see the rest, the details of the corporeal features of face and body.

FAITH. Faith—what does it mean? You don't see Christ or even feel him very much, but you carry on anyway, you still go forward. Is that faith? Or you notice that something is terribly wrong with the world and with your own life. But you go on anyway, even though something is wrong. Is that faith? I like the clear and objective definition of faith from my theological training, which takes St. Paul's expression "the obedience of faith" (Rom. 16:26) and explains it then as a submission of intellect and will to God who reveals himself. This is an elegant proposal if given half a chance. It proposes a risk in unpopular words, especially in the word *submission*. Yet it remains my choice to submit or not, and it is a choice to conform my mind and heart to something bigger. That's not a bad risk, not a stupid one. But how do I know what it is that God is revealing? Well, I find it in the witnesses, those who tell the story; and I put my trust in this. I put my trust in what the Bible tells. I try it out to see if it fits the world I experience. The content of this revelation is amazing. It is too good, and I am too small. I cannot come up to it. So, in the end my faith is the uttering of a question that is also the invocation of a name. Under my mood—God? Beneath my heart—God? After the reach of my eyes—God? Before or after the stars—God?

F ALSE IMPRESSION. It is a false impression, that easy sense we have that we know or can quickly know about other parts of the world, other cultures, other peoples. This false impression is created by the media and the Internet and rapid and comparatively effortless travel, given all the places we go and how quickly we get there. We should perhaps concentrate more on knowing and understanding better the place where we are. For example, I am here: Mount Angel, in Oregon, in a wide valley, on a hill, near the Pacific coast and the big ocean. It is today, only today; and I am here, only here. Things are happening, unfolding—bad things, good things, circumstances.

Nothing I try to do or think can abstract from where I am now. I must begin from here and from here search for the rest of the world.

FAMOUS PEOPLE. I was once asked to write a short essay on the most famous person I had ever met. Of course, I had no choice but to tell the following: The most famous person I've ever met is Jesus Christ. I have also had the privilege of meeting a number of other famous people, likewise justifiably renowned: Duke Ellington, Alvar Aalto, Pope John Paul II, Mother Teresa, even, years ago, Senator Robert Kennedy. But I have to say there is a qualitative difference to my having met and even managed to sustain a relationship with Jesus. Unlike all the others, Jesus is—just to mention a few of the qualitative differences—invisible, and he began to live his life on the earth centuries ago. In other words, he is not a mere contemporary of mine, *usually* a requirement for meeting another person.

How was it that I first met him? Well, I was raised a Catholic, and the story begins there. I know if I want to be taken seriously, I'm meant to denounce this fact and express my bitterness about it. But I have none. I'm meant to say that nuns and priests were mean to me, but for me that would be a colossal lie. In fact, it was my parish priests and the nuns who were my teachers in parochial school who first introduced me to the famous Jesus, and I shall forever be grateful to them.

The priests and nuns passed on to me what has passed in an unbroken chain through believing communities of Christians from the time of Jesus, two thousand years ago, to the present. What these communities passed on was the very presence of Jesus as a person still alive, albeit in a different form. This is a consequence of the claim of resurrection. Christians believe that this Jewish teacher, crucified under the Roman governor Pontius Pilate, has been raised from the dead by the one whom he called God and Father. The life he once lived does not fade away in a grave, its effects lessening with the passage of time. All that he ever did and said rises with him in the very body in which he once lived and died. His risen body is a new form, filled with divine glory, spiritual—which is more, not less. It is a qualitative difference.

My priests and nuns believed in such a Jesus and began to introduce me to him in a way that suited a little boy. I was taught that by coming into church I came into his presence, and I was told I could speak to him there. I tried it, and it worked. I met somebody— him. The church presence taught me his presence everywhere, and wherever I was, I could address him. Of course, as I said, he is invisible and doesn't speak back in any ordinary way. But my first teachers in the faith made me aware of a presence. That was how I first met him, and the relation has stayed alive ever since. Certainly, decades have subsequently passed, and I have had many opportunities to renounce all this. But my faith, begun as a boy, grew alongside me. In every phase of my life, I have examined again and tested the faith that was first proposed to me. It is still mine—no longer a boy's faith but probably only mine as a man because it was given me as a boy.

It doesn't have to work this way. People who have never known Jesus in their youth come to know him in adult life. As with all famous people, Jesus is met in different ways. I am recounting how it happened for me.

I mentioned that the relationship has stayed alive. So, this is not just a famous person I've met—like the others mentioned above—but a famous person I've come to know. This has been a great adventure, and it coincides with the adventure of my life. My whole life centers now around knowing him, around the desire to understand how it all works. I wonder, how can it be? Is it really he? Is this really God? I don't pretend that I don't doubt. But one thing I keep on doing keeps me thinking that—improbable as it all may seem—I am in contact with Jesus because he is risen from the dead and because he is God come among us in this completely unexpected way. That one thing I began as a boy. I come into his presence—aware that this requires my attention to a qualitative difference—and I speak to him. It works. Mysteriously I have thus met him and continue to do so. I don't hesitate to say that I love and adore him.

FEAR OF THE LORD. "Fear of the Lord" is a virtue highly prized in the Judeo-Christian tradition. Indeed, it is a kind of basis on which the other virtues can be constructed. "The fear of the Lord is the beginning of wisdom," the Bible often repeats. And, "Only a fool despises wisdom." But what exactly is meant in the Bible by "fear of the Lord," and is there anything about it that can "scare the hell out of us?"

I know that "scaring the hell out of" is just an expression, but here I want to take it to its roots, take it a little more literally than an offhand remark. Most good expressions that have entered the language usually carry a forceful meaning of which we are hardly aware anymore. That is the case here. And the point is, there is some "hell" in each of us and it doesn't come out very easily. Something really big is needed to scare it out. In the Bible, fear of the Lord will do that. But what does it mean? It's not as simple as being scared of God. Biblical wisdom is not that simple minded. Basically it means we take the measure of the difference between God and ourselves. He is big, and we are small. He lives forever, and our lives are like a flower that blooms in the morning but by evening is gone. There seems to be a fair amount of "hell" in us; in him there is none. Taking account of these differences is not meant to give us a neurotically negative image of ourselves. It just helps us to avoid a neurotically positive one, not based on reality. Becoming wise—and in the Bible this means living gracefully in reality as it is—begins with our taking the measure of the difference between God and us. Doing so, in fact, can cause a certain amount of being scared of God; but more than that, what it does cause is awe and reverence for God to rise up in the heart. For it is marvelous that despite the infinite distances that obtain between him and us, we are the object of his regard, the beneficiaries of his love. So, I find myself in contact through prayer with the Lord of the Universe. He draws near to me, of his own initiative. He reveals to me a little of his "mind" and "heart." And I am completely amazed, for all the while I feel at one and the same time his overwhelming infinity (fear) and his sweet and bearable closeness (wisdom). God comes close to us by means of what we might describe as a divine act of humility. From his high place he stoops down—so the biblical metaphors speak. There is an inverse proportion between how much God has humbled himself for our sake and his ability to be present to us in his being/essence despite our limited and sinful condition.

I know that not many people talk and think this way anymore. God is so humble that he doesn't force our recognition of him. But I, for one, want to witness to the fact that biblical wisdoms help me to live. Entertaining the proposal of biblical faith—that there is a Divine Somebody around bigger and far more worthy than I—lets me step into reality in the place and with the tone that is appropriate for me, who am not God, not in charge of the world, and only here for a while. I step in amazed and grateful to find myself here at all. I want to bow down in adoration before the One to whom I owe this gift. I fear offending his majesty, his goodness, his truth. And I fear this not because he'll turn around and smash me but because he is good with a goodness I could never match, and I don't want to presume upon it, take it lightly or for granted.

Presuming upon life, taking God lightly or not at all, thinking myself the center of reality—this is some of the "hell" that is in us. What really scares me is the prospect of an eternal hell. I know, it's not believed in anymore. But it's not as simple as our declaring it to be or not to be. The very possibility should terrify us. For what is hell? Not a vengeful, almighty God punishing us forever for having slipped up, but rather our living forever with the consequences of our choices. How easy it is to pretend that we will not be judged for what we do. And yet if we are?—well, this possibility frightens me.

FIFTIES. There are most certainly disadvantages to having been born and raised in the fifties, that cheerful and unreal decade. It means I was educated in the sixties with all its shallow ideas of how education works. Then I made my life choices in the Church of the seventies with its lack of gravity about the most serious matters. I hardly knew what serious was. Since the eighties, I have been trying to recover. It is not easy, but at least it is perhaps better than continuing on in whatever trajectory I might have been left in at the end of the seventies. Many of my age and slightly older are still following that original flight plan. What I feel missing most of all is the lack of a classical education. And yet mine was better than many others. Still, not to have Greek and Latin deep within me, to be deprived of knowing early in life the thoughts and emotions carried in these languages, philosophies, and literatures—well, then one is absurdly unequipped for life at a certain depth.

Even so, where does my regret come from? It must come from something I know, something I have learned; and so I can at least be hopeful in that I know enough to regret. Besides, this is where I am; this is my time, my only time. I would not be me without each of my decades and I cannot be other than me, even if I wanted. So, I sigh and say, So What?! So what if lots of stupid things have happened to me and I am consequently somewhat stupid?! So what if I cannot do much of what I admire in others?! I can nonetheless do something, think something, feel something. Connecting with things and people of other times, I can perhaps even do a lot. I don't mean a lot of things so much as a lot of living.

F IRST LOVE. When I was five years old, my brother and I burned our garage down. It was a big accident.

In the small town where I grew up, in north Idaho, the fire department was volunteer. This meant that a loud siren had to sound in the town to call the volunteers from their scattered posts so they could go rushing to the firehouse and then to the fire. The local radio would announce without delay where the fire was. This was so that, hearing the news, some volunteers could go directly to it. But the announcement was also made to satisfy the immediate curiosity of all in the town; for, of course, we all cared about and were interested in a fire.

My brother and my sister and I were having lunch with the babysitter when the siren began to blow. My brother jumped up and ran into the kitchen to turn on the radio and learn where the fire was. From the kitchen he could see the garage, which was a separate building from the house. He cried out, "It's our house!" Panic immediately entered into me. Running to the window with my sister and the babysitter, we saw huge flames leaping out of the roof of the two-story building. Yes, it was on fire! It *was* our house. Someone had seen the smoke and leaping flames and had reported the fire.

A crowd gathered on the lawn to watch the drama unfold. It was a stunning scene for a five-year-old boy under any circumstances, but the effect was ten times the stronger for it being "our house." This effect would be further intensified later when in my young mind I finally put two and two together and realized that what my brother and I had been up to in the garage earlier in the morning was the likely cause of this blaze. But in the first phase, that awareness had not yet dawned.

During this same period of my life, there was a girl in my kindergarten group whom I liked, and she liked me. I noticed I felt about her something different from what I felt about the other girls whom I also liked. I suppose it was a sort of first love, though I didn't know to call it such at the time. But the fire provided evidence of my unique feelings for her. I saw her in the crowd gathering to watch the spectacle, and I remember thinking, "Oh no! Oh no!" Just then she saw me and came running over excitedly. She grabbed my hand and held it as we both gazed toward the blaze. She was thrilled and asked in solemn wonder, "Whose house is it?" I realized in the midst of my panic that she didn't realize it was mine. So, trying to match in the tone of my voice her own pleasure at the flames, I said, "I don't know." But I could bear the pressure of this lie only momentarily. I snatched my hand from hers and went running off in a panic down the street to the house of my aunt and uncle. It was never the same again between us after that. Our love could not survive a lie. That was a good lesson. I learned also another classic lesson at this moment of my life: not to play with matches.

F OG. An odd fog seems cast over these months in which I've been in Rome, my first spring here in the new shape of the world after the events of September 11, 2001. The sun seldom comes through. I have no clear sense of time. What have these months been? Is this my life? Some vague force is urging on me the insight that the patterns and behaviors with which I have heretofore inhabited the world are no longer workable. Is that so, or is it just that I have grown used to them, and they now seem dull, but there is nothing more? "Get used to it" is the mean little inner voice I sometimes hear when I am struck by a quality of dullness in it all. Can this be the voice of truth? It seems too sad to be truth, and yet something about it is so insistent.

I keep describing my life to myself, amazed at how rich it is. I keep going over this because it is precisely this richness that confounds me when I have this feeling of dullness pressing in on me from all around. Very little is objectively dull. I live in Rome, one of the great cities of the world. I work with and am influenced by people, splendid people, from dozens of countries. I have friends whom I consider to be extraordinary people, and we pass wonderful hours together. How does the fog manage to creep in and render all of this dull? What is the fog?

I think often about the actual state of the world. It is the first time in my life that events have provoked me to a consideration of the real possibility of an apocalyptic ending. I've always resisted this for no better reason than that the likelihood seemed statistically unlikely that of all the billions of people who have ever lived, I should be alive to experience the end. But is this a real argument against the possibility of it occurring now? This idea of the end of it all presses itself more and more onto my consciousness. In any case, I am very sad about the world: wars, terrorism, greed, pigheadedness, hatred of Christ and of the Church. The charm of my life in Rome cannot cancel out this sadness, and I don't try to make it do so.

So, perhaps it is the condition of the world that is fogging my days. My life may be rich, but I still need a world around me in which to live it, and it's like it's not there anymore. What's there is cruel and crazy.

My prayer? God has been extraordinarily gracious to me through the years. Without my deserving any of it, he has somehow given me beautiful hours of prayer, times of contemplation of the Trinitarian mystery that leave me with a great sense of joy and wonder. Yet in what seems to be a completely irrational reaction, I feel now like I shall not enjoy such hours of beauty ever again. Why? There is no reason for thinking so, and yet the thought moves in me like a strange and strong intuition. I now feel very poor in prayer, even alone. I present myself before the Lord. I try to trust. There is little or nothing. Still, there is the memory and the knowledge of that past beauty. I use it, and it helps, but it does not seem very alive. Sometimes in prayer I sense that I am taken up into the wondrous exchanges of love between Father, Son, and Holy Spirit; but then I see that no thought or feeling could ever touch it; and so I have no thought or feeling; and then naturally I wonder if it is anything at all. Is it perhaps only me standing before nothing? Fog. Fog. Soft. Fog.

FORCES. I feel so many different forces in and around me. Some of these forces are conflicting, others simply different, yet in need somehow of being calibrated. There is the force of who I am, the man I have become and am still becoming. A direction is certainly set, a momentum carries me along. And yet, so many other forces make it unclear just how it will all turn out, forces in and around me.

I feel power and beauty in my body. This is new. New because it is not the power and beauty of youth. (I am over fifty now.) Like most in my culture, I suppose I have been the victim of unconsciously thinking that youth's strengths were the only ones. But slowly I have awakened—God knows how—to a power and beauty in me that comes from age, from my age. I am this person who feels these forces, and I wish to use them, not for anything in particular but for whatever I do. My body: precious, vulnerable, lifelong instrument of my soul! That's one force.

Another force—among many, many, too many to count and describe—is the force of my monastic vocation. It has been a long time now (more than thirty years) and it is always moving me along in generally rather rough-mannered ways toward some new point of arrival from which I must shortly thereafter again depart. Some of what appears in sharper relief recently is a band of detachment that cuts through a large middle of my life and leaves me now unconnected to much of what I was once strongly connected to: many people, family and friends, places I love, things I love to do, the monastery itself and the brothers. It is a desert place in which I hope for the visit of God, but I sense the wait may be a long one. Even so, I am also detached from much emotion about this. But I describe it as a wide band; it does not cover the whole of me. I am still connected, and I do have emotions about the visit of God. But these are not the middle, not the main thing.

Is there a main thing? I don't see one right now. I am aware that this may be dangerously close to being unhealthy. One can quickly lose his bearings in a land like this. But it is equally and perilously close to a new kind of health and a firmer grasp on the denser realities, on the spiritual realms. So this desert too is a force, and the force drives me more deeply into it.

Power and beauty in the age of my body and the constant interior movements brought on by the monastic way—I sense I am caught up in a great adventure, rather like being an explorer of places seldom frequented anymore. And it is not for myself alone that I go there.

FRIENDS. Many treasures are tucked away in the words of Jesus, "There is no greater love than this: to lay down one's life for one's friends. You are my friends" (John 15:13–14). Jesus' death is an act of friendship for me, and inside this realm, it is the greatest act of love possible. If I think about my own friends and how I would feel about giving my life for them, I see that I would be willing to do it, even if my having the strength to do so may be doubted. But I am willing.

And I see from this how much tenderness for me there is in Jesus, how much desire in him for me to live, to succeed, to continue in my mission. I think of different friends and imagine the particular feeling attached to giving my life for each, wanting each to continue living, to thrive, to be well. But Jesus' attitude toward me is like this! Only it is fuller, more complete, more tender and generous still. He no longer calls me a slave; he calls me a friend. In this love for me he makes known to me "all that he has heard from his Father" (John 15:15) and he makes it known by laying down his life.

This is the same context in which Jesus says, "This is my commandment, that you love one another as I have loved you" (John 15:12). This commandment is different from the command to love our enemies and perhaps greater in significance. It concerns friendship that is given by Christ. When I love friends in Christ and love them as Christ loved me—willing to lay down my life for them—and those friends know my love in this way and love me in return, then a tremendous circle is created, a communion which is nothing less than communion in the Trinity. This kind of loving creates a tremendous light for the mind and a speed in advancing in the understanding of divine mysteries; it creates a vision of all things cohering in a wonderful simplicity; it produces a power, strength, and energy to do good and an atmosphere in which things unhoped can happen.

When we think of our intimate, personal relationship with God, we tend to think of that kind of relating that comes in private prayer, in "our rooms with the door closed where the Father sees in secret" (Matt. 6:6). Of course, that is true. But there is also a terribly intimate communion with God that creates a terrible intimacy and communion among believing friends. This is a sweet, mystic communion of intense quality. It is, as the Apostle writes, ". . . so that you may have communion with us, and our communion is with the Father and with his Son Jesus Christ" (1 John 1:3).

FUTURE. The Christian idea of a future already accomplished is too strong a paradox for our overly logical way of thinking. In celebrating the liturgy the paradox becomes even sharper, where we speak of "remembering the future," and believe thereby that we somehow mysteriously enter already into it. This future tasted and touched then exercises its influence on the present. In the future we are already perfectly established in union with Christ, perfectly forming one body with him. To "remember" that is to bring it to some extent already into the present. Maybe some acceptance and understanding of this paradox can come from the simple experience of telling someone what I am going to do. For example, I leave persons I love, and so I tell them where I'm going and what I'm going to do. This sets us both at ease for living the present. Our culture has no account, no narration, of the future. So hope is very difficult. Christian faith does narrate a future and celebrates it now in the liturgy. This is, among other things, an offer of hope. All this applies quite directly to my own body. My actual present body does not have any completely satisfying meaning except in relation to its future transformed condition. No matter that it is virtually inconceivable: that my body is destined in Christ to share in divine glory forever is what gives meaning to my body in the present.

I learn all this by contemplating Christ, risen from the dead, in his human body. He said, "Behold I am with you all days even unto the end of the ages" (Matt. 28:20). Earth itself is a paradise, a heaven, for him. For here on earth he walks in a kind of force field that perfectly balances eternity and time, having received back in his human body and its place(s) on earth the "glory that was his before the world began" (John 17:5). Thus also our future is not elsewhere but in the world transformed and restored. "Then I saw a new heaven and a new earth" (Rev. 21:1).

GENERATIONS. Being a son. Being not my father. Being distinct, other, not him. And yet of him and out of him, and in that way being him, being my father by being his distinct son. One father. One son. And then this son becoming a father, with a son not him, a son being not him, being distinct.

As my father grows old, I trail him in that, refilling his forms, repeating his patterns, eventually featured as he once was, eventually so voiced, my breath the way his once was, his breath the way mine will be. But not him. Not at all him. Distinct. Other. Different. And in this way being my father, living and passing on the life of my father.

GERMS. We moderns tend to scoff at the credulity of the ancients who so readily believed in the presence of throngs of demons and angels invisibly surrounding them, anxious to harm or help, very much involved in their world. But how is it that we are so certain of the presence of incalculable numbers of dangerous invisible bacteria all around us and everywhere? Germs everywhere! Really? What faith!

GOD. Sometimes nowadays it is said that the name "Father" for God gives too strong a masculine image for our understanding of God and so should be eliminated or at least used alongside feminine names and images as well. Of course God is neither a he nor a she, and so no name and no number of rightly balanced feminine and masculine names can in themselves ever express who God is. But here I want to say why Christians use this name for God. Christians know God and address themselves to God in the way that Jesus taught. They do not invent their own way of addressing God and do not fashion for themselves a desirable version of a deity. All this they receive from Jesus. When Jesus teaches his followers the name "Father" for their most intimate form of address to God—in imitation of his own—it is just one more instance of the unfolding of the miracle of Christ's Incarnation, where the Eternal Word of God becomes flesh in a particular place and time. This is a miracle in which finite, limited forms are made capable of bearing infinite divine realities. The finite, limited form—in this case the name "Father"—bends under the weight of the divine reality it carries and is redefined beyond its limitations. If *Father* were a term of our own invention for God, then it could be justifiably complained that it is hopelessly lopsided and limits God to masculine categories, that it runs the risk of simply evoking the deficiencies of particular, earthly, failed and bad fathers. But in the mouth of the Eternal Word become flesh, "Father" is the finite, limited name he gave us that is a gate through which we pass into an infinite reality; namely, his own loving relation to the Source from which he himself is eternally begotten.

G OOD FRIDAY. There is a literal level on which the crucifixion of Jesus took place and could have been viewed. This is reported in the Gospels. But each and every detail of his dying opens infinitely into the mystery of God when that detail is proclaimed in an assembly of believers and received there in wondering minds and hearts.

Yesterday during the Good Friday liturgy, as the Passion was being sung, I felt myself entering more and more deeply into the scene, into the whole event. Toward the end, when I heard the words, "the soldier thrust a lance into his side, and immediately blood and water flowed out" (John 19:34), the whole scene somehow flashed inside me, and I saw everything first in its literal sense. There wasn't much to this part: Jesus' body virtually already drained of its blood, the soldier's lance drawing a little more, the immobile corpse unduly, momentarily disturbed. But almost at once—and precisely because I had seen this literal level well—the gesture and the moment opened outward into its fuller meaning: blood and water forever flowing into the sacraments that save us, into the sacraments that save *me*!

Perhaps it was in this same pattern of experiencing things that the evangelist himself originally wrote, and his experience is transmitted to me. This is as he says: "An eyewitness has testified and his testimony is true; he knows that he is speaking the truth, so that you may also come to believe" (John 19:35). It is enough for him to say it. When I hear his testimony, a flash of belief and understanding moves through me. I adore the mystery and exclaim, "My Lord and My God!" (John 20:28).

Although I discover this pattern in one verse during an intense moment in the liturgy, it perhaps could be applied to understanding the whole of all four of the Gospels in whatever they speak about. This would freshen the approach to what we mean when we say that the Gospels are inspired.

GOOD THIEF. In the hour of Jesus' death on the cross, which does not pass away, I try to utter with my whole heart the words of the repentant thief: "Jesus, remember me when you come into your kingdom." And from that same hour he answers me: "Today you will be with me in paradise." This "today" of the hour of the cross stretches out across my whole life and so helps me to see how closely and how soon I am connected to eternity. In my cross and in my slow dying across a lifetime, I am in a particular time and place; and yet at that very time and from that very place on that same day, Today, I will be in paradise. Every day I must be a repentant thief, and every day is the very day on which I shall be with him in paradise. The brief hour of my life is—all mercifully—the hour of Jesus' dying, which does not pass away.

G RACE. It is not what I do that will be significant and lasting but what I allow to be done in me by grace, by God's life acting in me. What I do is limited and will fade or fail. What grace can do in me and through me is limitless, coextensive with what God is doing in the world. This is unexpected and more than might be hoped for were it not for the fact that just such surprises are revealed in Jesus as the will of God for us. "The one who acts in holiness is holy indeed, even as the Son is holy" (1 John 3:7).

GRATUITOUS. I feel myself without past and future, and so my present is disturbed. Of course, I do have a past and at least something of a future, but I cannot feel them anymore or find them. I am astonished that I should be here at all, and my astonishment increases because I see no purpose to it. But need there be purpose? Perhaps not. And yet, to be here without purpose—perhaps that is the meaning of "gratuitous." I am here by grace. All is gift.

But God is gone. I go forward with faith, thinking that I can't possibly be right in what I feel; namely, that God is far, far away and doesn't care. So I do all the things that indicate that I think things are otherwise: I pray and I praise him. I thank him. Perhaps he is pleased. I hope so.

GREAT. The illusion that there is something important to do with one's life! Oh yes, I understand the point. Life is glorious, and we are marvelously made. But perhaps it is a question of the approach. When someone sets out to do great things, how much is accomplished really, and at what exorbitant prices? Maybe it is better to let go of the focus on great things as a goal, to live with hope placed in heaven, and then use well whatever time we find at our disposal. With the optic of that new amazement, something great may be done. But "great" will never mean a great me, a me that is marvelous and outlasts the short span of a lifetime. "Great" may mean something good done for others, something of value left behind. But I will vanish more and more. That is how it is, and with an act of faith and trust, I say also that this is how it should be.

GROOMING. I know it's not the main point, but when Jesus said, "When you fast, anoint your head and wash your face and do not look gloomy" (Matt. 6:16–18), we can see from this that Jesus was aware of and sensitive to the niceties of grooming. He would know from his own experience what it means to "anoint your head and wash your face." I love to think of him anointing his head and combing his hair and looking into some kind of mirror or into the lake to see if it looked okay. These are all wonderful details of the Eternal Word's expression of himself in the flesh. When he says, "Do not look gloomy," it means he knew how to look pleasant . . . or not. I like to imagine him examining his own smile, making sure that he looked approachable.

I want to keep alert in the Gospels for details such as these. They are precious to me. They help me to know what I am so weak in fathoming: that the Eternal Word became flesh. How could this be, how could this ever be? How heavy was the Word's beard? How long was his hair? How exactly was his smile? How were his eyes? How tall was he? How much did he weigh?

GYPSY. A scene I witnessed earlier today in the city helps me to understand what we mean when we say that we will pray for somebody and why we do it. There was a pretty little gypsy girl, perhaps twelve or thirteen years old. Suddenly a large man roughly flipped her on her butt and just as fast his hand was up her shirt where he pulled from her breast the roll of bills that she had pulled from him. The moment was necessary. It was harsh and cruel, and yet I think everyone who saw it was satisfied that this attempt at stealing had been foiled. The man was evidently carrying cash for the whole group of students he was leading around. But what I will remember now is this beauty: the color and tone of her young skin, her new breasts in a flash, her entire back (momentarily), and her streaming tears. I wanted to hold her. I wanted to say something. But I could not approach. There is no entry into a scene like that. There is no comforting a humiliated gypsy by someone outside her ring. Yet I know that I want to pray for her the rest of my life, and I want to be close to her in heaven. Will she be there? Will I?

HAIR. Auschwitz is, of course, impossible to write about, perhaps also impossible really to visit. It can't be taken in. I went out of a sense of duty, that I really must try to see this. I can only note that I went there and saw some things. Maciej and I did well to arrive early, at eight o'clock in the morning. We were able to go through it in relative quiet without too many other people around. It was hard enough moving through the cruel buildings, feeling the massive ghost of suffering. Thousands and thousands of their pictures lined the walls. Each one a somebody like me and those I love. But something snapped within me when I entered the room piled high with the hair of the women. It was in clumps and strands such that you could see the difference between one set of hair and another. You could see how it had been combed, braided, curled, set with pins. Who were they, these precious women—wives, mothers, daughters, sisters, friends—who looked at themselves in the mirror and, with great care, groomed themselves just this way this last time?

In the same room were clothes of tiny children, the

size of two- and three-year-olds. And then a huge pile of children's shoes. Darling shoes, with cute little buckles and straps. I kept looking at the various designs, trying to distinguish in each a different little boy or girl. Maciej and I were in this room alone and silent. I was grateful to have him to look at for a moment, to look in his eyes and see his equal horror across from mine, his equal disgust that this could have been done. Neither of us said anything.

In another room: thousands of eyeglasses piled into a mound. How precious seeing is to us. How clever we are to have overcome the problems we have with it. How wonderful to be able to read. Each set of glasses: a prescription through which someone received the world and loved it.

Crowds were arriving, and we left, returning quietly to Kraków. We arrived back in the beautiful city after passing again through the beautiful land. We ate a simple meal in an outdoor cafe that seemed all green for the freshness of the trees and grass that surrounded us. We go on living, and in the city moving all around us are the others who go on living. Why we are still alive and others are no longer—who can say? Who can bear the question?

HALLELUJAH. One of the great riches of monastic life—in increasing contrast to cultural patterns in America—is the living together of many generations side by side, day in and day out. In my community we have monks in every decade, from their twenties all the way to the their nineties; and we are all in it together, including dying and helping one another to die.

Father Anthony was having a long, drawn-out death. He was holding on very hard because, though weak and in pain, this was certainly better than actually dying. He kept wanting to put that off because he was so worried about getting it right, about coming before God with the proper disposition. Many of us would stop by and try to give him hope in God's mercy, urging him not to worry so much, as he no doubt had done for others during his long life as a monk and a priest.

It was Easter time and he had not yet died. In the middle of the night of Holy Saturday the monks were gathering for the long Easter Vigil that would celebrate Christ's resurrection. Brother James was the community nurse and was assigned also as a minister in the Vigil liturgy. He found himself vested in his long white robe, and he had a little time to spare before the ceremony began. So he decided to go by and be sure Father Anthony was sleeping well. He entered his room with a lit candle so as not to waken him. But Father Anthony stirred, and seeing the illumined figure, all in white, he thought it must be an angel, and so he at once exclaimed "Hallelujah!" thinking that might be the right thing to do. Brother James was taken aback, not only from the sudden unexpected shout but also for the strange word shouted; for in the Catholic tradition the word for the same is the somehow tamer "Alleluia," and in any case, it is not the sort of thing we monks generally say to one another. What exactly was Father Anthony meaning to convey? Brother James said softly, "Pardon me, Father?" The second shout was more tentative, though not all hope had been lost. Father Anthony said again, "Hallelujah?" Brother James came closer to what he later reported was a confused face; he said, "What is it, Father? Do you need something?" A flash of recognition lit up, or rather I should say dimmed, the face of the old monk for a moment, and he exclaimed with no small disappointment, "Ah hell, James, it's you!"

HAND. The ugliest hand I ever saw was stretched out in greeting toward me as I once boarded an airplane. It was to be a transatlantic flight, and my arms were full of various bags that carried things to relieve the boredom of the long trip. I had the good fortune that day of being upgraded to first class and was entering that rarefied world for the first time. I was boarding ahead of the hundreds of unlucky passengers who would follow after, and I was feeling grateful because I knew only too well what it is like to fly these long flights in the regular seating with the regular boarding process. So far there were only several other passengers sorting themselves out in the first-class cabin. I hardly took notice of them as I fumbled with my own bags, although I was aware that there was someone seated in the aisle across from the seat into which I was settling. As I was leaning over trying to place my computer carefully under the seat, this neighbor reached across the aisle and tapped me several times, not without a certain vigor, on my leg. Because of the angle at which I was perched in this moment, I couldn't immediately turn to answer the surprising summons. But I was tapped immediately again, twice and more vigorously. I turned to look, but since I was still cocked into an awkward angle because of the unfinished struggle with the bags, at first I saw only my neighbor's hand and arm as far as the elbow. Two things immediately struck me: one was the handsome quality of the sport jacket he wore, though, as I say, I saw only as far as the elbow. The other was his hand. I thought to myself, before I could check such a rude consideration, "My God, that is the ugliest hand I have ever seen!"

I was beginning to feel worried because generally I

don't like to talk much on airplanes, and now here was a fellow passenger who, it seemed, couldn't wait to meet me and stretch out a friendly hand. Bracing myself for the encounter with whomever it was I was to sit by for the next eight hours, when I turned to face him, I was completely astonished to see a chimpanzee dressed in pants and a sports jacket. Liberated from my baggage, I stretched out my hand to shake his. From the seat directly to his right, a lovely young lady then introduced herself as his trainer, explaining that he was a famous chimp who was flying to Rome for a gig he had in Italy. I could see in a glance why he was famous. He had charm and was nicely dressed; he moved with ease in his first-class environment. This was clearly not his first trip in this privileged part of the plane. He lightened the atmosphere around him, a lot more than I could do with my habitual determination to avoid talk on a plane. Even so, I was pleased to think of not having to sustain an extended verbal conversation with a fellow passenger. The chimp and I had established a rapport, and we would communicate from time to time throughout the flight. It was a pleasant trip. After a fine meal and several glasses of wine—the chimp had eaten only bananas—I settled back in my seat for a sleep. I glanced over to see the chimp with headphones on, and I fell asleep thinking how strange and wonderful the world is. From New York to Rome in just eight hours. Then the chimp to his tasks and me to mine. I go more lightly thanks to our unexpected encounter.

HAWK. There are hawks floating on the wind today. I love to follow their easy flight. I trained binoculars on one and decided that I would watch it for at least five minutes without taking my eyes off. On and on, round and round, gently up and gently down—looking, hunting. Beautiful.

HEARTS. Praying and singing on a Sunday morning, alone in my room and filled with joy, I praise the risen Lord. Suddenly my friend Peter M. jumps into my mind as someone who could understand what I am feeling and feel it together with me. In that being connected to him, even with my attention riveted on Jesus, I think I have some sense how heaven will be. We—a huge throng—shall be adoring and thanking Father, Son, and Holy Spirit, and *in so doing* we shall also know one another, discovering that the deepest joy and desire and secret of the other's heart is the same as our own.

HEAVEN. When the disciples of Jesus asked him to teach them how to pray, he taught them the prayer so familiar to Christians and used by them still to this very day, the Lord's Prayer. It is called such because the one whom Christians call Lord and Master gave it to them. Jesus answered the disciples' request by saying, "When you pray, say, 'Our Father, who art in heaven, . . .'" It is Jesus who taught this prayer and who prays it in an original, radical way. Christians believe that it is he who prays it within them. Or put the other way around: they pray it in communion with him. Praying with him they learn that heaven is not so much a place as it is a way of being. When they say, "Who art in heaven," they don't mean "who art elsewhere"; rather they are acknowledging in the divine Father his majesty and his sovereignty over the whole material order and the whole course of human history. His is a way of being before the beginning of creation, and it will be his way of being after the end. Heaven is meant to be the "place" of our future, where we are destined to share forever in God's way of being, in his before and after. When I pray this prayer and acknowledge a Father in heaven, I enter mysteriously somehow into the realm where I am meant to be forever, within Love's eternal flow. Paradoxically, then, in this moment, heaven is revealed as interior to me rather than somehow hopelessly beyond. And yet heaven placed within me is not my own doing and not a part of my original nature. Christ gives me this gift. In Christ heaven and earth are joined together forever.

H ÖSS. At Auschwitz, just beyond the double rows of electrical barbed wire, outside the prisoners' compound, is a yard with a simple gallows where Rudolph Höss, the *Kommandant* of the camp, was executed shortly after the liberation. I had read his memoirs of the camp, written during the months in which he was awaiting execution. Claudio Magris called these the clearest writing on Auschwitz in terms of establishing the objective facts because it is the only account completely devoid of emotion. Magris says, "A man who tells that story [Auschwitz] in anger or with compassion unwittingly embellishes it, transmits to the page some spiritual charge which attenuates the reader's shock at that monstrosity." Höss simply explains how difficult it was on the logistical level to do all that was expected of him. There were not enough ovens or sufficient quantities of gas, and the people were arriving too quickly and were not especially cooperative. (His wife and children lived in a house very near.) He is imperturbable in his matter-of-fact descriptions, which renders them virtually unbearable to read.

What were his matter-of-fact thoughts as he stood in this yard, looking out over the place he commanded, waiting to be hanged, not far from where he had lived with wife and children?

HUMILITY. I need to come back to it again and again: the humility of God. The One who is infinitely great makes himself lowly and small for our sake. To forget this or to pretend it has not happened is pride. I must come back to it again and again. Inscrutable.

IMPROBABILITY. To the improbability of the universe existing—yet it does—there corresponds the improbability of a planet like Earth existing . . . which, however, it does. To this improbability there corresponds the improbability of human life and consciousness existing on Earth, but it does. Then there is the improbability of me existing, and yet I do. I am writing these lines. To all of these improbabilities there corresponds, and yet infinitely surpasses, the improbability of God, Creator of the Universe, becoming incarnate in a human nature and revealing his whole being using the language of all these improbabilities. Yet it has happened. I believe in improbabilities, a remarkable string of improbabilities. Not in impossibilities, but in improbabilities.

INFINITE NOTHINGNESS. Three weeks alone in a house at the sea, and one day passing into another with the ocean continually pasted up before my eyes. I have very little sense of one day being distinguishable from the next or one hour of prayer to be told from another. Prayer? What a mystery! Sometimes I feel an urge to describe it, from curiosity, from a desire to understand it; but I waver between calling it intense or nothing at all.

Christ is so huge. I lay in bed in the dark the other morning and said aloud to him, "I am afraid of you." Of course, there was no response. I did not mean that I am afraid of his being mean to me, or something like that. I am afraid of his infinity, overwhelmed by it. I thought of him as the eternal God emptying himself and becoming one like us to the point of undergoing death. That death would have been a kind of negative infinity for him, an abyss of nothingness in contrast to his infinite being. How could he have done it! Sensing something of the horror of this, I felt that this infinite nothingness is a realm into which I could fall if he himself, who experienced it, does not save me.

INSTRUMENTS. In the *Rule of St. Benedict,* written in the sixth century as a rule for monks, there is a chapter called "The Instruments of Good Works." It is a list of some seventy monastic practices and tells us much about how monastic virtues and good deeds were conceived. One of the striking features of this catalog is that it begins not with anything specifically monastic but rather with the listing of the ten commandments and other key injunctions from Jesus addressed to all his disciples. When I first came to the monastery and was taught this chapter, I remember wanting to pass on quickly to the specifically monastic stuff. I have since learned that a monastery provides ample occasion for observing injunctions like "not to kill" or "to endure persecution."

INVISIBLE. Among many good reasons that God presumably has for remaining invisible, one of them seems to be so that his creatures—and especially the human person, his image—might step out into their own, that is, that they might appear in their own magnificence without being outshone by his own. Again, the humility of God and his gracious courtesy appear in this habit and arrangement of his. Thus, he can be pleased when two people are so absorbed in each other that they may not for the moment be thinking of him. He enjoys when we enjoy him in what he has made.

There is a lovely freedom in this that I think he would at least sometimes want me to derive joy from—the freedom just to live and take pleasure in things, without being especially religious. It is sometimes enough for me, and just what God wants, that I simply and carefully behold the other—the other person, the other thing.

This thought is applicable in its own way even to evil, sin, and tragedy; for in seeing any of these, I do so on the strength of God letting them be, his allowing freedom its consequences, his gracious waiting for our turning from foolishness. So sometimes I just live the tragedies without always reflecting directly on God and thereby still experience his retiring and even shy presence.

INWARDNESS IN THINGS. Suppos-edly we are made for God, for things absolute. But are we to go toward God at the cost of failing to notice that things in themselves are substantial, real, and engaging? Things exist in themselves, with their own proper nature; they exist as they are. There is a true inwardness in things, an essence to each. They exist in their own right. That all this should be the case surely also has something to do with God. In other words, religious stuff is not the only way to God. Focusing directly on him is not the only way. Thomas Aquinas said, "All knowers know God implicitly in what they know." Saying all this, I do not mean to deny my principle roots in monastic life and theology, but that doesn't require that I get all excited and exclaim, "Oh my God! It's the pope!" The pope fits in. I am grateful for popes. Yet even popes will turn the attention from themselves not only to God but also to the things of this world. "The beautiful quality of the light of your island!" I heard Pope Pius XII exclaim in a recorded speech to Sicilians visiting him in the Vatican.

JARRET. Bede Jarret was one of the best known of the English Dominicans in the twentieth century. He was a famous preacher and a prolific writer of books. But his fellow Dominicans used to marvel and remark that he never appeared to be doing anything. If you went to see him in his cell, he was usually doing nothing. If you asked him what he was doing, he would reply, "Waiting to see if anyone came."

J UDGMENT. The final judgment? How is it that we are all so sure nowadays that it is going to turn out alright? Such an easy, friendly thought. But is it correct?

K OLBE. At Auschwitz as we moved deeper and deeper into the camp, we eventually came to a building especially dedicated to death and torture: interrogation rooms, a courtyard in which people were shot, starvation cells, and cells into which prisoners were shoved and then bricked up. In this center of the horror we found the cell of St. Maximilian Kolbe. His holiness, his *being* love here in the midst of this, the presence of Christ in him—I felt none of these things there. It would have been a kind of consolation. Later perhaps. It was enough to mark the place, to stand there where he died and to try to remember why.

LADY'S MAN. In *An Interrupted Life* by Etty Hillesum, she is speaking about a man she admires and says, "I think most of us get the wrong idea when we hear the phrase lady's man—we immediately think of sex. He is a lady's man, true enough, but only in the sense that like Rilke, there is something about him to which women immediately respond and open up. And that is because he has so strong a feminine streak that he can understand how women feel—women whose souls find no home since men will not join them to theirs. But in him the 'soul' of a woman is given welcome and shelter. In that sense he is a lady's man, yes!"

What most moves me in this passage are the words "women whose souls find no home. . . ." I would like to have the wisdom and knowledge to give the soul of a woman shelter, welcome, and rest.

LAZARUS. I am like Lazarus, whom Jesus raised from the dead (John 11: 38–44); except I have got only half as far as he did. Lazarus was four days dead when Jesus, hating death, bid that the stone be removed from the tomb. Then he cried in a loud voice, "Lazarus, come out." The dead man came out, his hands and feet bound in the burial wrappings.

"Unbind him," Jesus said, "and let him go free." Jesus would do all the same for me, except I, when he bids me come out of the tomb, answer fearfully, "I can't. I'm dead."

L EGACY OF THE ENLIGHTENMENT. I wonder how much my sense of the absence of God is due to my being a child of these times and how much is just in the nature of things across many epochs. *From our times*: God banished from culture and public life, believers made to seem naïve and weak, science presenting us with too vast an expanse of the universe. The legacy of the Enlightenment, and all that. *From the nature of things:* because God could not be just another of the things on earth to be related to as one among others. He must be another dimension, and his absence points to this difference. It is absence only from some perspectives. From these his presence looks like absence. I try to think this through. These are interesting thoughts, and I think they are correct. But they do not always give me consolation.

L ITTLE THINGS. "Tante piccole cose, tante piccole cose . . ." This was Valeria's refrain at the age of ninety-five during our long conversation today. "Many little things, many little things . . ." She was remembering large parts of her century in Italy, smiling with gratitude, and explaining wistfully that the whole culture had been based on "many little things" that could give us joy. Examples from her conversation: slow train rides so you could enjoy the countryside; stopping at out-of-the-way stations, where there was a chicken coop and a garden attached; the sound of the station manager's whistle as he signaled the engineer to move out; the sunrise on the Adriatic, near Ancona, the sea so still; the family meals together and the special, practical yet elegant vessels that her mother had for these; the way her father tapped her on the cheek before she went out at night with her friends; linen on the table and knives that cut; cats instead of dolls because cats are alive.

Valeria is splendid, and I am fortunate to sit beside her in her reminiscing. That great culture of which she speaks is fading fast and all but lost, though perhaps parts of it could be regained by practicing. I need to practice letting little things please me. Otherwise I will finish among those whom Valeria sadly denounced: "No one is pleased with little things anymore." And this is very sad: she said she couldn't be as happy anymore because no one around her is.

LIMITS. An unbelievably beautiful spring day, coming out from under two months of clouds and rain. The green, of course, is intense: fields of grass or spring wheat and the softer-toward-yellow green of the just-budding trees. The view is longer than summer can grant when growth will be thick. I like especially the soft, long curve—all green—of the short hill in the near distance. The thicket of trees along its ridge is a dense wood, nothing budding there yet, looking nearly black in this day's light. This side of that hill the trees are opening, and so the mound I spy is through the still nearly bare branches. It will not be long—this is clear—until from here one will see only the thick leaves and nothing of the gracious curve of the hill behind.

What lies behind each thing that I see now? Life is springing up and will veil some things even as others come to the fore. In another season, life's leaves will fall and show again the once-veiled scape. It is an amazing rhythm. This is life. It is always moving, never still, always on the way, diminishing, coming back. And so I can think again clearly today about where and when and who I am. It is useful to take account of the fact that I am not everywhere nor in some other place but only here. This is my limit. But I am at least here, and I am grateful.

Not only am I here, but I am here *now*. That seems obvious enough, but accepting the fact with gratitude is not so obvious or automatic. That it is only *now* is another limit. It is only today, there will not be another. Stretch this fact out for a while and you have a lifetime. The *now* in which I am in a *here* is only a limited span. I am not in another century, another epoch. I have only this day. It is given me. I may be given another or even many more, but one thing is certain: a day is not forever and no amount of days ever could be. Praised be the One who from his Forever gives me one day in the shape of whose limits I see, conversely, One to whom I cry out, "O Illimitable You!"

LISTENING. Benedictine monastic values are perhaps best summed up in the injunction with which the *Holy Rule* of St. Benedict opens: "Listen." Monastic life is a way of life devoted to the practiced art of listening. St. Benedict says, "Listen carefully, my son, to the master's instructions, and attend to them with the ear of your heart." In the immediate context in which he is speaking, St. Benedict is referring to listening to the words of the Lord as expressed here in the words of the *Holy Rule*. But monks through the centuries have learned from that listening that the range of that to which they listen will grow ever wider. Among other things, monks listen to their place; and everything they do there, everything they build and plan, wants to promote this listening. This listening becomes an exchange between the place and those who live in the place.

So, for example, at my monastery one listens to, and with the ears of, the heart, attends to a hill, to many trees, to wonderful views, to the light of the passing hours of day and night, to the seasons and their weathers. And why? Because monks are meant to listen for God everywhere. Above all they will hear him in his holy word, the Scriptures, which all the monastic practices are meant to promote and put into action. But this very word teaches monks that creation itself is already God's message. It teaches also that living in time—call it a little piece of history—Christians are meant to live their redemption by building and planting, working and praying, creating a culture that speaks their Good News into any number of forms that will celebrate it and share it.

LOSS. I'm thinking all the time about people, their differences, their greatness, their squalor; I'm thinking about cities and about wars. I'm thinking of problems, and I also think of things like wine or mountain lakes, lovely things. I feel like I'm moving forward with a new understanding of something. But of what? Of life, perhaps?

It has become very hard for me to "work," but I can't tell if this is progress or a problem. Work here means writing an article, preparing a class, reading students' papers and helping them. I can hardly do it, or I only do exactly as much as I must. But this is perhaps to the good, for I am thinking all the time, even if I am not making any direct progress in theology in the sense of reading and learning things I don't know about.

I have many poems rising up within, but to write and refine them is also the work I seem unable to do. I just quietly hold the thought of the poem and then move on. Eventually, of course, that poem is lost, but then another rises up and another, and this for the moment seems better than writing. True, if I were to write the poem, it would not be lost. But that all things are passing and are lost is my fundamental thought and insight now. So writing too is loss. If it is done at all, perhaps what should characterize it is some reverent sense of inhabiting this loss, this world where all things are lost.

LOVE OF ART. When people decide to stay in a place for their whole lives and dedicate themselves to building up that place into a monastery that gives glory and honor to God, and when those people know that after them others will carry on what they have done, there arises rather naturally as a dimension of the whole project a desire to do things beautifully, to create a place of beauty, to create beauty that will last. This has happened in thousands of monasteries through the centuries; it is why monasteries have contributed so much to culture. In addition to the beauty sought in the buildings and the landscape, the arts contribute greatly to the creation of a beautiful place. Music, for example, renders worship beautiful but also extends from there into many other dimensions of life. The plastic arts are important also in the church, but likewise they appropriately adorn every other place of living and activity at the monastery. Even furnishings and vessels are desirably beautiful and made to last. Beautiful language—poetry—is happily an inevitable dimension of the monastic way. Beauty in a place creates a momentum to refine things even more, just as lack of it can impede the momentum. Thus, in all that is undertaken and planned at any monastery, the conditions for creating beautiful things must be considered a necessary ingredient of the project.

LUCKY. I lead an unusual life, and I am lucky. I live away from "the action," and often enough don't even know what the action is. Yet I hear its voice in the near distance. I know that on this account, in my case, I can be closer to what is real—not because I hear the noise but because I am not doing so much of what so many others do. But the noise reminds me that I am near them. I recognize the density of reality in something like my six weeks in Paris: living in the center of the city with a wise man, inhabiting his ideas, praying with him. Or, in another city, just two hours of talking with Milosz, but all the reading that prepared for it and now follows—this is living as concretely and as fully as I can imagine. Or my friendship with M., where none of what we do is exciting or fun in the way that society conceives of these, and yet he is a real companion in soul and mind. We are constantly interchanging things. And now I am thinking of all this in a quiet house in the country, where with several other friends, we try to be faithful to offering up our simple prayers, to choosing our reading well, and to spending some time together in the evening that will be enriching for each. I cannot ask for much more.

MARIA IN TRASTEVERE. The September sun is beautiful: bright and cool; it has a (slight) calming effect. I have arrived to where I set out to walk: the church of Santa Maria in Trastevere, one of the most beautiful in Rome. The newly cleaned mosaics on the outside are gently played on by the sun. Colors all around the piazza, including the colors of people's skin and clothes, seem so graced today, so full of divine play and pleasure. Inside, under the force of the apse's mosaic, I remember with a certain nostalgia my first time seeing it, more than twenty years ago, around this time of the year. I gasped with delight seeing Mary seated on the same wide throne with her Son, seeing his clear centrality but also the clear centrality of them both. When I first saw it, I remember the immediate grasp I had of myself being associated with her on that throne. I feel it still, and it is such a joy to look up and say, "Blessed is the fruit of thy womb." That fruit extends outward from her Son to include me and everybody and everything I saw this morning. That fruit is this morning as I was seeing it. All of Rome is that fruit. Rome is the unself-conscious celebration of an immense history, the unself-conscious celebration of life itself, the unself-conscious celebration of the Christian mystery. For centuries Rome has been attempting to express beautifully "the fruit of her womb."

MASS. Alfio is the old gardener who has spent all his long life in this part of the Umbrian valley between Todi and Perugia. When on Monday I teasingly asked him why I had not seen him at Mass on

Sunday (for he is always there), he told me that he had gone instead to Collelungo because it was the patronal feast of the church there. He said, with a thrill that made his body shudder and shine, "C'era una messa infinita, maestosa." It was an infinite, majestic Mass. I tell this because, by my telling, the reader now knows a truth that was true before the reader knew it; namely, that Alfio belongs to the world and that the world is full of such beautiful souls. Each soul, a singular secret. Each lasts as long as someone lasts to tell of them, then passes. We last awhile, as long as someone bothers to tell. But we are there, beautiful in any case, even if unknown.

MATERIAL. In the monastic tradition *material* and *spiritual* are not conflicting poles or opposite ends of a spectrum. True, the spiritual is the nobler of the two and the object of the monk's quest; but the material is the Spirit's instrument, its glad and willing servant. It transcends itself in the uses into which it is caught up. And so, by care for their material environment across every conceivable slice of their lives, monks are enfleshing and expressing an otherwise elusive spiritual story. This interplay between spiritual and material, between creation and a little piece of history, unfolds into values that the monastic tradition has articulated and which, among other things, affect the architecture and the entire arrangement of the physical environment. These values find expression and direct the design of virtually everything that is built, every arrangement that is undertaken, every decision.

MESSAGE. Things have a message. All things do, if only I know how to hear. Cups, lakes, clouds, trucks, dogs, desks—anything. Everything! I have this image: I bend over and put my ear to anything at all—say, to the side of a couch—and I listen very carefully to the quiet stream of the Eternal Word of God, holding the couch in existence, giving himself to me in the world that surrounds me. Each thing: a door through which the silence of God breaks into some particular, partial expression.

MIDLIFE. I am still guided by the experience, many years after it happened. I step into the scene again and live it as if present. I am walking in a forest alone near my thirty-sixth birthday, and I remember again for the first time in years, probably because the way the light falls through the trees is the same or because the sound of the wind in them is similar, I remember wonderful walks in the forest when I was a boy in Idaho, walks with my big dog in a forest near a lake. She was a wonderful dog, a perfect pal. We must have done a hundred miles together. And now maybe midway through my life, I see how much I owe her still. It was something she and I discovered together when I was a boy and I've had it ever since, but I am remembering it more clearly now. I see how it's been in everything since she and I split twenty-five years ago. I mean this amazing sense of feeling accompanied, of not being alone even when there's no one else around. It was like the forest herself was Somebody and my dog and I were this Somebody's friends. But not exactly only the forest as Somebody. It was like everything, the whole world was a Somebody—Somebody who loved me, Somebody who knew all my thoughts and feelings and cherished them. My dog taught me to believe in it.

I'd walk the path, and she'd run wild everywhere this side and that side of it, and when she'd cross over, sometimes she'd check in with me by jumping up on me quickly before passing on or lick me maybe or wag her tail joyfully as she rested a few steps beside me, but her insistent, regular, faithful returning to me even while running and sniffing almost everywhere was her saying to me something like, "Isn't this wonderful, isn't it wonderful that we're here with Somebody and Somebody loves us!" And from her bumping into me I gradually came to believe it and I've been walking on and believing it ever since.

So here I am walking, nearly thirty-six years old, and I catch myself walking with that same joyful feeling that I had as a boy. I begin to think about all the years in between and what they mean. I have to say that Somebody is still my friend and loves me. I am saying to myself what my dog crashing into me used to say. I say: Isn't this wonderful! Isn't this beautiful! Then when I say it, there is a great She in the forest with me: my dog the she, but other shes too, all the other shes and hes of these intervening years. I stand still a moment while the beautiful faces of people I love pass over me through the trees, and I think how many good places I have been, how many good people I have loved and how many have loved me. And I think: I'm always walking. I've walked down streets in cities, lots of them, lots of pretty cities. I've walked on beaches all up and down and on both sides of a couple of continents. I've walked alone and with people I love. I've met strangers and it was good and interesting. I think about my work—teaching—and the special way in which I've come to love my students. In fact, I was studying for them before I went on this walk and what I see now is that I really only want to teach them what my dog taught me, how wonderful this all is. And in all my walking I think I'm just wanting to spend time with Somebody again. I like to walk with people I love because it's like continuing on with what I started with my dog.

I'd like to live another thirty-six years and be seventy-two some day. I want to be seventy-two and still walking like I walked when I was a boy with my dog. A great She tugs on me in the forest and invites me to follow her. I'm going to go. Maybe we're going another thirty-six years, maybe not. What I see now is the next step and a little of the path in front of me. I see the sun setting soon, but She is inviting me up the mountain and the light will be there longer. Right now it's so much gold that I think maybe it will always be light on this mountain. Gold. Somebody is gold. Somebody is light. Somebody who has always loved me—yes. Somebody near and yet far—yes. Here and always—yes. Yes. Yes.

MISTAKES. From Romano Guardini I have this huge and useful insight about a subtle but deadly mistake in the modern way of viewing things. We view *Nature,* the *Subject,* and *Culture* as domains independent of God. God in effect does not exist, or more accurately, God has been killed by man. And yet Nature, the Subject, and Culture are what is distinctive in modern man and all these are potentially an advance over the medieval worldview, which referred this world too radically to the next, such that it did not take this world with sufficient seriousness. In any case, these three as they could be positively conceived would look like this:

Nature: the reality of that which is given and the seriousness of its objective determinations. Only not to take it as the ultimate reality.

Subject or the concept of Personality: this as indicating the possibilities and the limits of human beings. Something wonderful! Indispensable new concepts. Only not to presuppose a presumptuous autonomy.

Culture: this affirms that the world is confided to man in a special way, to an almost terrible degree. Only not to think that man is master of himself.

When we human beings view God as another, as *the* Other *par excellence,* we cannot bear God's presence, which is too overwhelming as other. Understandably we rebel. We must kill God, eliminate him. God is dead. But—again, Guardini's insight—God is not the Other. God is God. Of all other beings, we can say, one by one, "That one is not me, therefore it is another." But this does not work with God. In fact, that this does not work with God mysteriously expresses the essence of God.

MONASTIC. I should study and read and perhaps also write primarily with a view toward keeping my own relationship with God intact. If something is produced for others as well by my working in this way, so much the better. This is the monastic way of doing theology.

MOOSE. Czeslaw Milosz died in August of 2004. I was having a little vacation in north Idaho at Priest Lake when news of his death came in an e-mail from a friend in Poland. I had read Milosz voraciously for the last four years, had met him just the year before, and had been writing to him in the months before his death. Priest Lake is one of my most favorite places on earth, filled with memories of my happy boyhood there, and for this reason I suddenly experienced it as one of my strong connections with Milosz. (I have always found myself moved by his poems and essays about himself as a wide-eyed boy discovering the beauty of the world in the river, the copse, the fields around his home.) The evening of the day the news came—in Idaho it was still the day of his death—some friends and I took a long ride in the boat at sunset and talked mostly about "Inheritor" and the great author of this poem. I was holding forth about how this short, twenty-line poem is quintessential Milosz. We were also drinking whiskey, which I imagined would have somehow pleased the aged poet. As we moved quietly along the smooth-as-glass surface of the lake, we saw in the near distance a large moose, crowned with a stunning rack of antlers, swimming from one side of the lake to the other. We slowed our boat so as not to frighten him and waited to watch him come ashore. What had been only a large, peculiar head moving through the water, suddenly loomed a towering beast, shook itself, and then disappeared calmly into the woods. I took it as a little parable, enacted by nature, of the great poet's passing: strange, huge head, moving from one shore to another, towering figure, shaking something off, slipping away into the dark thicket.

After that, I found that I could not read him anymore. Often in the coming weeks and months I would try again, but I could not connect. Every time I would pick up the poems, I was reminded that there would be no more of these. Never mind that I had hardly begun to sound the depths of the thousands that he left behind. I somehow found it unbearable to face the fact that there would be no more coming. I could only remember that moose, that antlered head, disappearing into the forest. A disappearance sudden and definitive.

The spell was broken at last in the final days of June in 2005. As I was leaving Rome for three days in the Umbrian countryside, on an impulse I put a volume of Milosz poems in my bag. Unaccountably, I found I was able to read him again and did so for hours of each day. I had broken through something. I don't know how or why. It was like the sudden appearance of a moose.

Perhaps the lull had been a kind of period of mourning imposed by the nature of things. Not that I was mourning for Milosz personally all this time. I did not know him well enough to suffer his passing in that way. But now that I am back to reading him, I feel something appropriate and proper about the nearly twelve months that passed in which I was unable to read him. He needed to lie still in death, all his poems silent for me; and I needed to absorb this huge fact, so much a subject of his writing. I see a difference now in how I read the poems that I have read so many times before. They still stand in their own right whether the poet is dead or not, just as any great work of art has to be great whether we know its author or not. But I am helped somehow by the perspective of his death. I experience it as a strange redoubling of the perspective I gained in reading him after my several long meetings with him and the intensity of our discussions. He is gone. It's final. There are no more poems. But there is still his voice: I hold our conversations in my hand.

MOSQUITOES. There are probably billions of mosquitoes in any given season around Earth, and yet there are probably more stars. And when you think of how much is going on in and around a star, even a fairly average one like our sun, then to consider that there are more of these massive, complex stars than the endless parade of comparatively less complex tiny mosquitoes on any given summer night just in the one place where I am—well, then I ask where on earth are we when we are in the universe.

MUSIC. Music as reconciliation of life's enigmas. As consolation for its sorrows and disappointments. As love and compassion. As hard-earned joy. Music as Truth, terrifying in its beauty. Highly structured, very mathematical and yet—or rather, *thereby*—very emotional.

MUZZLE. The dog I had as a boy stood at a height where her muzzle was level with my bed. This made for effective early morning communication. I could easily be informed when she wanted me awake and up. Her wet muzzle would be jabbed into my face accompanied by the dog equivalent of what we humans call whining. Then she would step back slightly and move her feet rapidly up and down in place, making a clicking sound with her claws on the tile floor. The first jab would inevitably wake me, and she would observe closely the telltale signs. Then I would always feign sleep, and the evident lie frustrated her. The next jab would be preceded by whines and the clicking paws. She would come in harder this second time and also begin to lick. I would shift a little, trying to lend some credibility to my fake sleep. But she knew, and she knew that I knew she knew. Suppressed whines, continued clicking. I would eventually turn and look her in the eye. Her entire being began to wiggle with the joy of a new day and of our being together.

This has had a profound effect on my life, and I want to bear testimony to it. One of my earliest strong thoughts and insights into the world is admiration not only of the dog and her humor but also of the divine Creator's ingenuity and humor. I am, among other things, placed in relation to all kinds of animals who inhabit this earth with me and want to live here too. They are full of delightful traits, and by means of some of their emissaries, I am united to them all, enjoying the differences and marveling at the possible points of contact. The wet nose on the snout of a dog and her lively eyes at the end of it—the whole animal kingdom comes and calls me awake for another day in this our place.

NATURE. For many days now I have carefully watched the developing dawn from the two windows of my room—my perch—at the corner of the top floor of the monastery. Along the full length of my eastern horizon there stands high the wall of the Cascades, the uneven black line along which the light slowly comes on. Each day is magnificent, unique, and if I think in a certain direction, terrifying. For of so many millions of days in this place, how relatively few have been viewed and pondered by a man? What, then, is their beauty for?

On the eastern wall of my cell is the icon of Christ. I try to pray to him as this is happening, to pray to him as the Lord, as the Word through whom all things were made (John 1:3; Col. 1:16). In the logic of such faith each of the millions of days is his creation, his doing. But my question becomes then even stronger. Why was Christ doing days like these countless times before this one in which I seek him in prayer? When that question strikes, I lose him; he vanishes; it seems impossible. Can Christian faith really be? This is my terror, my sadness, my confusion. I stand all alone before this spectacle, deeply aware of its beauty, but I understand so little.

At length the bell rings and calls me to Lauds—the precise, definite, historical psalms of lauds, prayed in the hour of Jesus of Nazareth's death and resurrection, which does not pass away. What has this to do with the dawn still developing beyond the church walls, another of the nearly infinite number of dawns? I do not know. I do not find the connection. I throw the psalms up in the direction of the eastern sky. I paste them up against the gorgeous colors of the vault. Under them all is a prayer something to the effect of, "If it is you, O Christ, then show me how it is you!"

NINETY-THREE. When he was ninety-three years old and not far from death, Father Martin said to me, "It's no good waiting forever." He meant that he was ready to get on with it, ready to die. Shortly after, he looked up and, reflecting on time stretching itself out in the way that it does, he said, "I came to love you more and more." Then turning back to the prospect of his death, he said, "It's like being thrown out of a plane in the dead of night. You have no idea where you'll land. All you can do is receive the sacraments and hope for the best."

NOTHINGNESS. First we must consent to the nothingness of our existence. Then we can enjoy every presence that appears before us. Doing this, the *nothingness* is gradually transformed into an overflowing *everything*. Thus can I live at every moment the unspeakable wonder of creation *ex nihilo*.

NOWOSIELSKI. In a parish church in a suburb of Kraków there are beautiful icons by Jerzy Nowosielski, the fourteen stations of the cross telling the story of Jesus' walk to Calvary. Numbers 12, 13, and 14 end in the sanctuary and are part of its decoration. They are much larger than the others. There is a small but certain resurrection in the top right hand corner as a finish. In virtually all of the scenes Christ is pictured with the other two who were to be crucified with him. He is always clothed in a long red robe, while the other two are naked except for a thin white loincloth. Seeing them all three in station after station delivers a very strong sense of Christ's solidarity with the condemned. When Jesus is stripped of his garments, all three are lined up virtually naked against a wall that resembles the wall at Auschwitz against which prisoners were shot. In the fourteenth station where Jesus is laid in the tomb, his ribs and stomach have the outline of crosses. His body is nearly black, but these crosses glow with a faint, deep red light, as if the mystery of the resurrection were beginning slowly to work its way through him. It is just above this that the much smaller scene of resurrection is placed—in a different realm. The church is cared for by Franciscans, and so between the station that shows lots of motion in hoisting the three condemned onto their crosses and the big crucifixion that dominates the sanctuary, there is an icon of St. Francis with his stigmata, and in bright red, the many-winged seraph, covered with multiple eyes. Francis's participation in the mystery of the cross is inserted between Jesus and the two others who die with him.

OFFERING. I sometimes feel stupidly disappointed that God has not given me some greater work to do. This is not vanity, or at least I hope it is not. Rather, it is just some strong desire to be useful to God, to be involved in something great like so many of the great things God's grace has brought about through the centuries and is doing in our own time. What is stupid in all this is that it draws my focus and center away from something God *has* given me to do and what I so longed for when I first came to the monastery; namely, to exist primarily for the praise of his glory, to have prayer as my work and my profession. So, to find that center again and to be grateful for it: to pray here in the monastery in the way that is expected of a monk and then to hold myself ready to do whatever else God may ask.

In fact, a monk is called to a life that is mostly hidden—hidden from others and eventually hidden even from himself. As such it begins to seem to the monk not to be much of an offering to God. I, for example, can experience my offering—faithfully living the life of the monastery from day to day—as something rather dull. I'd prefer to be doing something else, but that's how I know that it's an offering. Being disappointed is no sign that this is not what I am called to do and be. Indeed, according to the monastic theory, this is precisely how it is supposed to work: you offer to God the not knowing, you offer the not doing something greater.

My silly disappointment and my restlessness is not unlike the apostle Peter who said to Jesus, "Lord, I will lay down my life for you." Jesus knew that what Peter offered then was nothing he could count on. He is kind to Peter, but he also exposes him. "You will lay down your life," he says; "No, you are about to deny me three times." I do not need some greater work. I am fortunate to have what I have.

O'KEEFFE. In, of all places, *Hemispheres,* United Airlines' magazine, over Montana, returning from Rome, I read of Georgia O'Keeffe, and I find a suggestion for poetry in something she says of her paintings: "Seashells and rocks and pieces of wood that I like. I have used these things to say what is to me the wideness and wonder of the world I live in." I find this so suggestive; it makes me want to do something in words like she does with a cow's skull or the insides of an iris or some other flower.

Flying over Montana is sweet and strange. There are many little clouds separated from each other, each cumulus; then very square, irrigated, man-made (and in that way beautiful) patterns of fields; and then the wild irregular patterns of sun and shade pasted across the land by the varying clouds.

I think how earlier in this long day I was in Rome, and now I am looking at this. The quality of light in North America is so very different from Europe, from Italy, where I can even feel now the difference between Adriatic and Mediterranean light. I love these lights. Even so, North America, Montana, heading west—we shall come over Idaho soon: this is my land, this is my first light. I love these differences, of course. But for me, I am penetrated now, surrounded by the most familiar light, flying through the air near my first point of reference!

OLD. A strong man I know is dying. He is old. His whole life has been a struggle, filled with his and others' pain. That he is still alive in his nineties is owed to chance. He has survived scores of close calls. He has always been strong both in body and in mind.

Among those who die slowly, from a lingering sickness or just old age, I have seen different kinds of death. Some are peaceful and serene; others can be a fierce physical and spiritual struggle. Often the strong cannot die easily. This is not from lack of faith. It perhaps stems from habit. People who have become strong by being made to go through demanding situations had always to exert a lot of control to hold things together. And since dying really is a slow losing control, such people can experience this quite dramatically. It is a tremendous shock and a comparatively new experience. Yet it must, of course, be accepted, must be learned.

In each one of us there is a light, our essential self, which survives death, indeed, which is released by death because this essential self cannot be identified with our bodies even if it is intimately joined to the body throughout our life in the body. As we are dying, we should concentrate on that essential light and move toward it. I want to say this to the old man, whom I love. And I think, when my time comes, I will need somebody to say it to me.

OPENING. When I think of the significance of my life or of any life, however great and influential, it is all nonetheless horribly, painfully insignificant against the backdrop of the whole of human time or the material size of the universe. And yet, my little life is in fact a space opened up for me by God out of the nothingness of being. God has opened this space for me, and he places me within it to be and to act. It is this decision of God that gives my life value, not the comparison of it with other things that are larger and more vast than it. In fact, this is a love story. God opens up out of the nothingness a space for me to be. He creates me out of love and for the sake of love. And should I sin, he opens up out of that nothingness a new space for me out of love. In some ways this story of love is bigger than the whole material universe and the vast story of human living.

OPPORTUNITY. To fail with style, to transform a shipwreck into an opportunity.

ORCHARD. Simple impressions summarize whole decades of my life. A butterfly is my childhood. Green trees against the blue sky: the loneliness of my youth. Yellow dry grass: all of it together. I am walking in the orchard. It is Sunday. From somewhere low inside me I feel my whole life surging up, decades of living and of experiencing things; and the surge gathers into a capacity to see clearly and to *be* clearly; and for some few minutes I am there walking, completely alive, completely joined to the history I have lived, to everyone who has crossed it, to all whom I have loved. But I am joined as well to my future, which moment by moment comes rolling toward me as I enter it step by step. Christ is here, but not like religion, not like a prayer. Everything I am experiencing and the whole of my life is being joined into one presence and person across from me, though not staying across from me but invading me as I step into it.

OYSTER. If I declare that the world is my oyster, that means I'm at home in it and find it full of desirable things and people, that I'm here to enjoy myself. So, is that something I as a monk can say? Is the world my oyster? Joining a monastery is not the usual response of someone who discerns the world as his oyster. For me, in fact, things worked rather the other way around. To my surprise, my *cloister* has taught me to feel at home with the *world*. Life in this world, with all that it casts up before us for our enjoyment—is this not something truly wondrous and to be grateful for, even if it is not my only home and does not define my entire destiny? All the same, there is a deeper advantage in the oyster association. The original expression can be traced back to Shakespeare. In *The Merry Wives of Windsor,* Pistol, in answering Falstaff, exclaims, "Why, then the world's mine oyster, which I with sword will open." In Shakespeare's time, cutting open an oyster was an image for laying difficult matters bare. May I dare to claim Pistol's image to describe my reflections here? It is what I am attempting, that is, if not entirely to lay bare, then at least to pry open a little some of the difficult, mysterious, beautiful matters of the world. The world: my cl-oyster, a splendid pearl!

PACIFIC OCEAN. At the ocean the scene is lonely because the expanse is vast, nothing is named, and very little human history has happened here. Things are just fine here without any of us human beings around.

The ocean is not only beautiful, vast, mesmerizing. I find it also terrifying. Not in the sense that it might overrun its limits, climb up the bank and sweep me away. No, terrifying in the sense that it is just always there and rolling in and out in its huge way as it has done just like this for tens of thousands of years. I do not know the long-term geological history of these parts, but there is a definite sense of it all being and looking like this, apart from the comparatively few puny houses, for thousands and thousands of years. Every day only this—the tides in and out, storm and sun and shore and sand, the gulls feeding and flying so, the sea lions unchanged in their habits during millennia. It is terrifying. Things are just fine here without any of us human beings around.

PAIN. How am I to account in my heart for the fact that pain far worse than mine is oppressing people by the hundreds of millions? That a comparable pain like theirs may touch my life one day or may not? Is there some hidden law at work that explains these differences?

PARADISE. The question, or at least the tone with which we tend to ask it nowadays—"Why am I here? What is the purpose of my life? What is the meaning of history, of this whole created order?"—is a question that arises with a sting as a result of sin and the distortions in our perception that sin introduces. When life in this world with its difficulty in following moral principles seems to me like a lot of bother on God's part just to unite us to himself, then I know that I have lost the original wonder and insight of Paradise. For if I could somehow walk again in the first Paradise, I would experience the magnificent abundance of the created order and the thrilling promise of a history wholly guided by God. I would experience this as explainable only by Love. Only Love, only divine Love, with its limitless delicacy, could and would create a world like this and place in it his own image and likeness. Image and likeness of God—that is what I am and that is what we are.

So there is a sense in which our salvation from sin will show itself as a restoration of the wonder of Paradise, where life is no longer experienced as something of a bother and where doing the will of God is not experienced as a burden and a chore. No, just as in Adam I sinned, so in Christ, the new Adam, I am come to a new life: a being in the body and on the earth in such a way that the only explanation is Love, living a new history that derives entirely from him and whose characteristic mark is entirely doing the will of the Father in joy and trust.

PARIS. When I am in a city and sit quietly and alone in my room in an effort to pray, I somehow begin to feel all around me the thousands of people, and it just seems odd that I should sit quietly in the midst of them. From my window in an inner court I see at least a hundred windows of other apartments, and I can't help thinking something like, "Well, here we are on top of one another." There is nothing wrong with it; there is even something touching about it. In any case, it is hard to ignore; and it takes over my prayer; and I'm not praying; I'm thinking about all this. Maybe I go off in this direction because I was raised in a small town and in another country, and it is so different from where I find myself now. Where am I when I am not in Paris?

PENINSULA. Italy as a peninsula—you feel it when you're there, even if few of us feel much of anything like that anymore in our culture dominated by technology. But with a little attention the effects of the peninsula can be noticed all around. One sea never far away and the other never much farther, land thus taken less for granted than in the great, vast expanses of Europe and Asia. You can feel Italy by contrast with what it feels like when you're way up inside part of Europe—for example, in Poland, around Kraków. Then there is the Oregon coast and the huge Pacific. You are not really seeing or feeling that sea if you do not also somehow feel a huge and gorgeous continent at your back. This is very different from looking at one or the other sea in Italy, which is a peninsula.

PHOTO. I am gazing now at a photo of Natalie and Nathan, my niece and nephew, ages eleven and eight. Will those beautiful children live to be old before they die? Yes, of course, I hope so, hope so with all my heart. And so then, how many further ways of looking will come across their faces? What of what I see will fade? What of what I don't see now will come into their glance? Can people who look like this grow old? Of course, we know they can and will, but, hard though I try, I can't see how when I can stare like this at the fresh faces of the young. And did people, old now, once look this fresh and beautiful? They did, of course, we know that, but how hard it is to see. And all the while . . . within . . . invisible . . . it is always the same me, the same she, the same he. Our looks go on changing around a solid, invisible core.

It is a comparatively recent development for the human race, this possibility we have to stare at a face in a photo, including our own. It is far different from a mirror, where what we see is always present, always right here. A photo is the past and elsewhere. We can ask, "Did I once look like that? Is that what my sister looked like that day? How pretty she is! Is that what we looked like together?"

Then there are the photos of the dead, our beloved and well-known dead or the countless unknown. For me it is a deeply unsettling experience—also mysteriously beautiful—to stare into the photographed face of someone who has since grown old through many other stages of life and then died. The faces of the young survivors of the great world wars. The beautiful young women ready to dance in the cabarets. Children playing in a park in the 1930s.

P IMPLE. When I was in my late teens, I found myself in the lucky situation of being able to stay for three weeks in my brother's apartment in San Francisco. I had determined that I would learn about the world while there, and so I set off each morning systematically walking the streets, planning in this way to see a good deal of the city and to drink in its spirit. I did so, but I am not writing about that here. I am only remembering a funny line that an old philosopher-bum said to me in a short conversation we had on the upper end of Grant Street. He had managed to condense into one short phrase what apparently was his basic insight about the mystery of life. It was enough for him to repeat this phrase, interspersed with sighs, not especially dramatic. He kept on saying, "I'm just one pimple on the ocean, one pimple on the ocean."

I knew his meaning, of course, but what caught my attention was this use of the word *pimple*. It seemed such a striking way to make the point that each of us is so small when set up against the vast world, the universe, in which we find ourselves. (From the dictionary: "A small hard inflamed spot on the skin, or anything resembling a pimple, esp. in relative size.") At the time I was not especially moved by the content of his thought. In the late teens one feels big, not small. But I did appreciate his manner of expression, and I have quoted him often since. Gradually, because of the memorable form of expression, its content entered my consciousness as well; and I realize now the importance of living with this insight.

Now I too pronounce it as an insight, as a means of taking my bearings: I am but one pimple on the ocean. Behind me stretch the billions of years in the place where I now am. Before me stretch the planet and the universe—lasting, lasting, lasting long after humans are gone. If I try to bring things down to a human scale, I am still only a pimple, a particle, a blip. One civilization succeeds another. Billions of people like me alive before and alive now . . . for a while.

Is the God of Jesus possible in all this? Is Jesus as God possible? Has God in Jesus really come among us as another pimple on the ocean? This is what we believe. But put this way, the content of Christian faith appears even more amazing than anyone could ever have imagined. In one pimple on the ocean the infinite being of God is revealed!

POET. The Poet as one made to see, really to see, and then to say, really to say. But what if nobody listens? It has probably always been that way. So this too will be a part of what is seen and said. Yet the poem uttered has its force in the world, like the word the Hebrew prophets once proclaimed. Israel believed that the prophetic word pronounced, which came from God, was an event, a three-dimensional event, and not merely indifferent sounds issuing from the throat. Such an event set other events in motion, moving in a way they would not have moved without that word. Reason to fear the prophetic word or to hope for a good one! What really has force in the world is right living, the living that is event. This sounds like I may be speaking of morality. Of course that is a part of it, but I mean something much more pervasive—the whole of every day and every hour gracefully seen and then lived and perhaps occasionally also said.

POLAND. Wherever you go—surprising personal connections, and all things eventually touch. Only a little attention is required, and you can begin to trace the trails.

It was late in August when Maciej and Daria and I left Bydgoszcz and drove to Gniezno, the old capital of Poland when it was first being formed of Slavic tribes in that region. It was there in 966 that Duke Mieszko I accepted Christian baptism, which effectively introduced Poland into Christian Europe. In the little city there is a large and beautiful Gothic cathedral where St. Adalbert is buried. He was around in Mieszko's time as bishop of Prague, where he was not wanted. He left and went to Rome where, though a bishop, he wanted to live like a monk, which he did at Sant' Alessio on the Aventine, just down the street from where I live during the five months I pass in Rome each year. He eventually died a martyr on mission in Prussia, but not before he was sent by the Pope from Sant' Alessio to Hungary to found the great monastery of Pannonhalma, where I am scheduled to preach a retreat in the coming year. Recently, thieves or a peculiar type of religious zealot sawed off the silver head of St. Adalbert represented on his tomb over the high altar, but it has been replaced with another one, and you wouldn't know the difference. Sawing the head of a saint's tomb seems a bit sacrilegious, though not as bad as Czechs and Poles having wars with each other through the centuries over who should have the body of St. Adalbert. The Czechs soon forgot that they hadn't wanted him in his lifetime and stole the body from Gniezno and brought it back to Prague. With more war it was returned to Gniezno. The things that people fight about! The things they steal!

In any case, I knelt down and prayed at the tomb of this bishop, monk, and martyr. I prayed for all the people I know named Adalbert. That's two. (In Polish *Adalbert* comes out as *Wojciech*. He is patron of Poland, and the name is common there, and so Daria and Maciej could think of more people to pray for.) Then I prayed for all the Poles and Czechs and that the Christian faith would remain strong in these lands. I prayed for my friends and neighbors on the Aventine and also for my old students who used to live at Sant' Alessio, especially Luca, who died when he was thirty, and Remo, an Italian who now lives in New Hampshire and works with orphaned boys.

From Gniezno we carried on to Biskupin, which is the site of the discovery of one of the oldest civilizations on the European continent, extending back some 13,000 years. There are more substantial remains from the Bronze Age, some 6,000 years ago: a city of long log houses on an island in a lake. The place as place is by no means stunning: rather flat land, well cultivated now, a small lake and not in any way dramatic. But nonetheless, there is something moving in thinking that in this place people lived some 13,000 years ago. The day we were there was the day that Mars has not passed so close to Earth in 60,000 years. So, something was happening there in the air that had never happened there before for any of all those people. A fierce cold wind was blowing on this August afternoon, and summer was already over in these parts. I know it's not connected, but I somehow felt that the wind was blowing so hard all day because Mars was so near. Naturally the sky was cloudy that night, so there was nothing to see. But I consoled myself by thinking how far away again can Mars get before I get my next look at the sky?

At the end of our outing we came back to Daria's apartment in Bydgoszcz, drank tea there, and ate the sweets we had bought the day before in Torun, the town where Copernicus was born. The best sweets were the ones that hundreds of bees had been swarming around that day in the shop when we bought them. I noted from Daria's window that she was similarly positioned in her house in relation to the Bydgoszcz prison as you are in walking along the Roman Janiculum in relation to the Regina Coeli prison. I told her of the Roman custom of the women singing to the prisoners at night from the hill for their comfort and suggested she might do the same. What a comfort her singing would be for those prisoners, whoever they are.

PRAYER. I speak in my prayers to Mary and say: You, the mother of Jesus, are the mother of God who became flesh for us. Beg him not to abandon the work he set out to do, beg him not to give up on the race of which he became a part. Remind him of his *Huge Deed* and tell him that for some reason we need more help so that its force be extended to us. Tell him of me who, though a sinner, recognizes the beauty and generosity of his plan to create the earth and the life of human beings upon it. Tell him that there are many sinners like me who nonetheless still see and believe in his plan and who beg him for strength to be lifted up from their sins. Ask him, Holy Mother, if maybe the repentance of a few might not be counted as the repentance of us all. Wasn't that in fact what he himself already did when as the sinless one he became sin and begged mercy from his Father in the name of us all? So then, tell him, Holy Mary, that never has his race needed his attention as it needs it now. Implore him to forget not the work of his hands.

PRIEST. One evening Nicolas (age nine) interrupted a dinner conversation that was going in quite another direction and announced, "I have a question." Then he turned to me and said, "What's it like as a priest to say the words of Jesus at Mass, 'This is my body.'?" I knew that he needed as clear and complete an answer as possible and that he expected it to be brief. So I told him that you could feel in that moment Christ completely taking possession of you and that you experience his total love for the people, his desire to give every bit of himself for their well-being. You feel it especially for the people who are there in the church but you know also that this love is for the whole world, for everybody and for everything in the world. In another direction you also feel in yourself Christ's love for his Father, burning like a roaring furnace. You understand that the reason he is offering his body and blood is because in this way he wants to honor his Father; he knows that the Father wants him to offer himself for the world in this way; and he gladly does it, so full of love is he.

I could see that Nicolas was made happy by this answer. The smile that spread quietly across his face when I had finished betrayed a wonderful understanding, a kind of knowing satisfaction, almost a "Yes, I thought so." He had told me the week before, with tears in his eyes, that he wants to be a priest when he grows up.

PRINCIPLE. What is so frightening about the present course of human history is that there is no principle of unity any longer operative. Countless thoughts—a good many of them noble and true and sincere—lie scattered over the face of the earth but with no force that can any longer pull them together and purify them. Only in Christ can this be found. Good apologetics would demonstrate this and (re)awaken the hunger for it in the human heart.

PROCESSIONS. Christians believe that what God once accomplished long ago for his people is always available to each subsequent generation of believers. That availability is made active principally through a liturgical reenactment of the saving deeds of God. One way of understanding what God has done for his people—and thus what is still available today—is considering the divine action as a series of processions in which God himself leads his people to salvation. Thus, there was the *procession* out of Egypt through the Red Sea at the Exodus, the *procession* of the forty years in the desert and the giving of the Law on Mt. Sinai, the *procession* across the river Jordan and into the Promised Land. All these processions shift keys in Christ, who leads his faithful followers in *procession* along the path that he himself trod: in the exodus from death into the Promised Land of eternal life, an exodus from this world to heaven.

Monks are always having processions. As a community, whenever we go from one place to another, we don't just do it helter-skelter; we go in procession. We process into church; we process out. We process to a meal. We process to our cells. We process to the cemetery. We process around our property. I am glad for all this marching about. Of course, it could become too formal; we could make it overly serious; and then it would just be weird. But I experience it as an extra in my life, something in my day that I would not have were I not a monk. And so I am reminded again and again that I am not just vaguely moving through life. In my life I am inserted into the definitive procession of Christ. I am part of a huge story, a huge movement, a definitive exodus. I am going somewhere.

P ROSE. On the level of a linguistic metaphysics, prose is always *within* poetry and springs from it. Poetic talk is the more radical, the more original. Prose is commentary and interpretation of the more dense poetic word. But we forget this poetic frame, and we take up poetry to interpret it as if it were prose.

PSALMS. For decades now and every day within them I have been singing the psalms—scores and scores of them, hours of each day. I sing them all—every one—and then start them all over again. I have become a long line of words, an arc of sound, a tone that tries to span the dividing spaces that keep the world from what can save us.

I do not get across. I call from the far side. I stretch all my being into the narrow lines that say those right and only words, words that every day trace our fall and point the path of return. I crawl over every word. I grope my way over and around every syllable, each phrase.

QUALIFICATIONS. Often I am kept from acting in important matters because I feel that either I do not have the qualifications to be involved or I wonder what power I have to effect a difference. On this latter point I should reflect on how the smallest ingredient introduced into a situation can eventually produce a significant change. Thus, to act! To act even in a small way on an important matter! As for qualifications, I should work to be as qualified as possible to deal with the matter at hand; and if I cannot be largely qualified, then I can act in a small way according to what qualifications I may have. On the deepest level it is not qualifications that matter but that God accept the offering of our action and bring it to completion, for next to God and his purposes we are all, in all matters, severely underqualified. Yet he uses us, and not just on the side of the scene but in ways that are critical to his purposes.

Thus, always to act, when by life's funny accidents I find myself in a position requiring my action or inviting it. To act in a small pure way, detached from how I may look in so acting and detached from my own narrow views of what the outcome should be. To act, as an offering to God, letting him use my small contribution for his wondrous purposes.

QUEST. As a writer, a poet, a teacher, here is what I would wish to be able to do: to express a thought or insight or to describe some thing or person or event with absolute precision and clarity of thought and at the same time, and as part of that very expression, to suffuse the whole with the deepest of feeling, with intuition, with a sensitive grasping of the "co-inhering" of all things.

I have this desire (again) after praying before the Blessed Sacrament exposed, and in a long moment I somehow understood with a fair amount of clarity and theological precision the relation between Christ's risen body and his Eucharistic body and the relation of these to all bodies. In one grasp I felt the resolution of many intricate questions, and I know that with time and effort these could be unfolded. But this grasp was likewise suffused with feeling, with emotion that was inextricably part of the thought and that nuanced and guided it. There was adoration, wonder, joy, gratitude.

Only a work of art or only theology of a most beautiful kind could approach an adequate expression of all this. I feel so weak and ill-prepared. I can conceive the task with precision, but I cannot accomplish it. The prayer before the Blessed Sacrament only occasioned these reflections, but it is not a goal to be applied only to subjects of so profound a nature. This would be a principle to apply to virtually anything and everything—to think clearly and deeply and to do so with love.

QUESTIONS. Does Nature feel herself being Nature, or do all the rhythms and cycles, now launched, just continue to rumble dumbly forward? If it is only the latter, then all this might basically be a very brutal story. Take, for example, the flight of a bird—does it *delight* the bird; or can it only be delightful to us? There are thousands upon thousands of things—like trees, clouds, rivers, cliffs, glens, gorges—that are delightful to us, but are they delightful to themselves and to the other creatures? When a cougar passes a cliff, does it delight in its beauty and in the quality of the clouds beyond? There seems something like delight in many animals who appear at least to enjoy their own kind—lion cubs frolicking with daddy and mommy or puppies playing among themselves. Others seem to exult in what they can do: the leaping fish, the speeding gazelle. But none of these species gives evidence of having a grasp of the whole. They do not reflect on why they do what they do, and they do not think forward to their deaths.

This raises a big question: What is the whole scene of the world for? Why the thousands upon thousands of years of these exchanges and cycles of creatures, beautiful as a whole to none, delightful as a whole to none, except to us human beings in the midst of them? The biblical answer moves in two steps. First, God creates each different creature for its own sake. Each exists because God wills it to exist, and its very existence proclaims his glory. Then in a second dimension, on a different level, the entire scene is for our sake. All these beautiful things were created so that God could lead a different kind of creature into his garden and say, "Look at all this," and this creature, different from all the rest, *could* take delight in the whole of it, just as God also does.

This explains a lot, even if not all. However, this

answer is hardly any longer allowed in the culture as an explanation, and so a person needs real strength of character and even courage to live by it. The dog lobbies and the rock lobbies and other such lobbies think it means we want to cut down all the rain forests. They caricature our belief, though admittedly the biblical doctrine has been badly misused. But when the qualitative difference between human beings and other creatures is banished from the culture as an acceptable explanation and ordering of the world scene, then

despair seems a predictable result, coupled with the effort to avoid it by means of cheery distractions. Despair, because without acknowledgment of this qualitative difference, we are only a part of it like all the rest, and we will inevitably drift toward an implicit acceptance of the meaning of our existence as just fitting dumbly into the cycles. If we deny the qualitative difference, we might as well admit that anything like *our* delight in the flight of a bird is a false human mollifier, a sentiment unworthy of brutal reality.

That said, I do admit to a problem in accepting the biblical explanation. It presents difficulties today unknown to those who were open to it and lived by it in the past. The extent of the space and time of the universe as now measured by science is so vast that explaining all of it as being for the pleasure of human beings seems a bit extravagant, to say the least. I too am stumped before this. Beautiful Umbrian night under all the stars—what for? And the animals around me in the dark—what for? What, if anything, do *they* feel about the stars?

RAÏSSA. I felt myself cooled by the shade, the trees of green, and the other greens by which I was surrounded: cedar, fir, oak, fig, mint, blackberry, lawn. It was Sunday afternoon and I was reading *Raïssa's Journal* (Raïssa Maritain) under the cedar tree just next to Brother Claude's icon studio. Raïssa. There are several pictures of her in the book, one where she has just turned twenty. She is beautiful, a bright soul shining in a young face; and this visual image subtly accompanies my reading, my letting myself be led by her thoughts.

Suddenly I hear a loud, clumsy thrashing sound coming from the grotto—below me, to my left, out of sight. I stand up to look, and spot a deer, a doe, who in the same instant spots me and so fixes me and herself. I match her stillness and stare. We are two animals, suddenly brought together. There is no hostility, though there is caution, more from her part, of course, than from mine. She is the first to move, and when she sees that I don't, she is calmed. Eventually she climbs to the rim of the grotto, all the while keeping me in sight. In her new position, I see that by moving only my head I will put a tree trunk between myself and her line of vision. I make my move, and she immediately stretches her neck round the other side of the trunk. I am seen again. I move back. So does she. And so on. Five or six times. I set a slow rhythm, twenty seconds or more between each shift. What absorbing theater!

This was a game you don't get to play too often. There was for me an unusual joy in it. But more, I felt simply the deep mystery of another living being, a being for whom eye contact with me was, at that moment, absolutely vital. She stares at me from a certain distance: the doe, Raïssa, Being Itself. There is distance and a certain caution, but I connect. Here, under the shade of a cedar tree in the thick summer.

R ECORD. Everything that is ever done is "recorded." I do not know how or "where," but what I mean is this: nothing that ever happens can thereafter be undone. It is henceforth a part of things; and its consequences, however great or small, begin to ripple outward and make their effects felt. I'm not referring only to the realm of human actions and even there to our more decisive and intentional actions. I am referring to everything, everywhere—to the spider and the fly, to the tree in the forest, to the deer eating berries. It is all recorded in the sense that, once done, it is what is there and becomes part of what has been. The human mind can note or trace only the smallest fraction of all this. But the divine mind grasps it all, contains it, understands it, loves it, glories in it, records it. This gives me hope when I feel paralyzed into inaction by the immensity of my context and the consequent ineffectiveness of what I would do. No, instead, no matter what I do, if I perform any gesture, however significant or insignificant, it enters thereby into the great *what-has-been* and begins to condition the *what-is-now.* I perform not so much before other potential observers, myself included, but above all before the Divine Recorder who sees all with fond care and will never forget.

RELATIVITY. The importance of being convinced of the relativity of earthly things. Hard to stay in this thought.

RELIEF. Nothing that exists is necessary. But everything that exists, does. Tell me why, and I shall be much relieved.

RESTLESS. A house in Umbria where the beauty of the rolling hills, many crowned with little towns, presses peace in through my eyes, presses great peace; and it is impossible to be in this valley without thinking of Francis and all his saints. Their famous joy. Their peace. I imagine a Francis here or one of his little brothers. I think of them responding to this place where I am, to the colors of land, stone, olives, sun flowers, wheat, trees—the response of their renowned simple hearts and merry prayers. Was it really for them anything like I imagine it? Or did they have my struggles?

What are my struggles? Well, I feel that in my soul I cannot come up to all this beauty, that I cannot match it in my spirit. To say that I feel alienated from it would be too strong, and yet there is some kind of distance between me and what surrounds me. I associate what surrounds me with Christ, and I cannot come up to it in a way that would be worthy of it or worthy of him.

In this I am perhaps just another sorry instance of sorry contemporary human beings. Ours is a world and a culture that has lost the natural sense and feel for the presence of God. More than we realize we must be ruined within by the genocide and all the stupid wars that have marked the last hundred years. How am I to act in this natural and beautiful place when I know what monstrous things my race has done and is doing?

Is it right for me to be alive when so many others have been so cruelly cut short in their lives? I think of how many wonderful people I know, of how deeply good and uniquely beautiful each one is. I don't know any monsters. So who are these people who do monstrous things? How does it come about? Are the good somehow also guilty?

I am not content to do interesting things, know interesting people, and have people interested in me. I think I ought to have a more heightened sense of how I belong to all the rest, to the rest of humanity, to the rest of history. But why? Where does this restless urge come from?

It is possible, I suppose, that it is a sort of Christurge in me. In any case, I wonder if it might be. I mean by this that Christ within me renders me restless. It is his Spirit, his movement of grace within me, his interior formation project for my spirit which does not allow me to rest content with my own interesting life and its many lucky days. These too, of course, would be part of his project; but in that case they are in part a foil against which to stir up the restlessness.

This is an interesting theory but hard to know if it is true. I think I hope it is. It makes some sense of things, including this feeling of the absence, or at least the distance, of Christ from me. But it may not be true at all . . . in which case what does the absence or distance mean? Maybe nothing. That would be quite an absence, quite a distance.

Thinking and writing like this is my practicing the virtue of hope. As the Apostle says, "hope is not hope if its object is seen." So, to say it all more directly: I hope for Christ, though I do not see him, though I do not feel him. I hope that all the awesome mysteries I read about and study about are really true and will be realized not only in me but in all humanity. I hope for interior joy and steadfastness and intensity of communion with Christ like I hear about in the lives of the saints. Oh yes, and I do hope also for a continuation of my interesting and lucky days. I hope good things for the many beautiful people I know. I hope to be a good friend to my friends, to honor them well with love and affection.

Moving ahead now into the coming months of my life, it looks rather likely that rich days will continue to unfold before me. I will be in Paris with G., then in Kraków with M., and return from there to Rome. Then I will be back in Umbria staying again in this same place. Yet a part of me hesitates to step forward into these days. My most spontaneous instinct is to stay put. But I should make these trips, and the very going will pull me out of centering in myself. It will unsettle me and crack my walls and defenses. Between the cracks I hope the light of Christ will shine. I hope to grow larger within. I hope to bear my inner poverty and fears with a graceful touch and even with good humor.

RESURRECTION. That flash of light and that opening into the divine infinity through all the particulars of Jesus' life and death—all that *is* the resurrection, in which the one who is raised is this Jesus who lived this particular life and died this particular death.

Yet Christ as risen seems at once strongly present to me and simultaneously absent. It is frightening. I somehow experienced his risen presence strongly in the Easter liturgies and in the celebrations of the Eucharist now during the week after Easter. I use that experience to pause in the day and make contact with him. He is there, as Lord, present and sovereign. Yet it can also be like nothing, and I can feel so very alone. There is a sense that I could never possibly get it right and correctly detect the real, actual way that he is present to me. It cannot be how I imagine it might be. It could not be explained by the kinds of thoughts I inevitably shape as I try, rather naturally, to understand it. So, I practice letting go and letting him be, hoping that he will show himself as he knows best. It is then that there is nothing, and in that nothing I have this hope: that he is somewhere between the lines of it. Even writing about this now, it is off; it is like trying to trap him between the lines of what I am writing. So I cut off with a plain prayer: Jesus, Lord, I am a poor man. Come to me. Let me know and share in your glory.

Within these thoughts there lies a theological response to the kind of critical exegesis of the Gospels that sees the various stories and words as, at least in part, constructs of the evangelists or of the first communities. Such a view can make believers nervous and scoffers gleeful, because the conclusion seems to be, "Well if they are constructs, then it's all just made up. And why believe in what ancient communities made up to suit their own purposes?"

From any ordinary perspective the Gospels may in fact be exactly that: constructs of evangelists and communities. But what is ultimately operating in the hearer, even through the construct, is that flash of resurrection light which henceforth determines, as the final and ultimate content of the Gospels, a definitive access to the infinite divine life by means of the limited, earthly particulars of Jesus' life.

RISKS. Life anywhere is going to be a strain, and much of it comes from the fact that on so many levels we are unhealthy. And then we live in unhealthy ways, with damaged structures. On the surface there is much in monastic life that can threaten to increase the problem. Celibacy is such a risk: all of us men living together and tempted often in the most subtle of ways to take compensation for our supposed sexual sacrifices. A monk can get himself into quite a state.

A state—that's an interesting concept. Who is the ultimate author of the state of the monk, God or the devil or the monk himself? Perhaps it begins with the devil and then at some point can be taken over by God, and the monk decides into which of the two directions he will lean.

One of my states is sometimes a great sorrow and a great loneliness, even a kind of anguish. What is God's will for me? What am I to be doing with my life from day to day? Is what I am doing all that God wants? Though I ask these questions in openness while praying for light, I often seem to have very little. The darkness becomes a "state," and I am left with nothing but the vague sense that possibly the struggle with this unknowing is what God requires of me as a monk.

I say "possibly," but a whole life can be wasted in this way, and venturing it is a perilous risk. My version of the unhealthiness inherent to us all can increase; I can feel it growing within me, concisely expressible in the well-worn but precise phrase "going crazy." But while I go crazy, is there some way in which God's will can be done in me and I in fact come at a deeper level to a spiritual health that is at first known only to him? I cannot say, but this is my hope. Surely the expression "offering up one's life," which we use so often in our talk of a monastic vocation, can in some cases mean this kind of offering. In religious life some offer themselves for the missions, others for the service of the poor, others for education or for care of the sick; but the monk's offering is perhaps meant to be more raw, more radically fundamental: not offering oneself for anything, just offering oneself, like Abraham offered Isaac, like Jesus offering himself during hours on the cross when he experienced himself abandoned by the Father. At first glance, there could be no greater waste than the death of Jesus. But look! The infinite fruits, the glory, the sheer majesty of what he did, hidden while happening but changing the whole cosmos from that point, henceforth and forever.

ROAR. The ancient Romans thought of a crowd roaring as an awesome and mysterious moment. An eerie daimon of unanimity suddenly and unpredictably sweeps through thousands of different people all at once and binds them into a same emotion, causing to rise up from them this huge sound as evidence of its presence. And just as quickly the phantom departs, though the sense of its presence and the emotion linger. We are no longer inclined to consider a crowd's roar in these terms, but isn't something needed to urge us to experience with greater wonder such an amazing phenomenon and to give us some means of measuring its mystery? There we all are: though part of a crowd, each is in his own little interior enclosure until suddenly we are all together and all at once on our feet and roaring sounds, sounds unintelligible in themselves but forming together a great expression of unity and communion which most certainly is peculiar to our race and to which there is nothing comparable among the other animals active on the planet. Would that God himself might suddenly sweep through the crowd of humanity gathered in the arena of the world and we, all of us together, would roar our excitement and gratitude at the unexpected communion brought on by the visit!

SAINTS. What or who but the Catholic Church remembers so many, many men and women long since dead, remembers them and calls them by name, counts them friends, and recalls their deeds? Catholics in Oregon, the far west of what in centuries past was called the New World, remember and talk about Francis and Clare, Augustine, Gregory, Catherine, Gertrude, Cornelius, Clement, Philip, Elizabeth, Luwanga, Miki, and thousands and thousands more. This is just some measure of the respect and gratitude for one another that we learn from the Church, respect and gratitude destined to last an eternity.

S HOOTING STAR. What is wondrous about a shooting star is that its visual impact is delivered with utter silence. It is an image of the life of the body going out and being replaced by the invisible and silent life of the Spirit. Silent. Invisible. Darkness. But wonder in my heart.

S LAIN. What slays me about the present predicament of the world is that the solution is available, truth is in our hands. But we are all looking elsewhere, doing other things. God has come in Christ. Wisdom and power to do good are given us. And instead we busy ourselves with things that move us in other directions. Whence such perversity? God does not force the gift that can save us. He seeks to persuade. We refuse.

S LAVE. I feel it useful to note, however plainly, that now, at the beginning of Lent, I am very much struck by a desire to enter deeply into the mysterious inner place of Christ's willingly "being a slave"— which is not a bad way of understanding virtually everything he was up to in his life and death but which is said explicitly in these very words in St. Paul's Letter to the Philippians at Chapter 2, verse 7. Actually, I cannot enter his pattern with anything near the proportions of the distance he crossed, passing from (again, St. Paul) "the form of God" to "the form of a slave." Yet even so, his pattern is available to me on however smaller a scale. I would want to understand my main work in this light and insert studying, teaching, and writing into Christ's self-emptying pattern. Then these have nothing to do with advancing a career, but rather are meant to be a service to my students. And let me add the ideal: even a very menial service to them. For this I need, among other things, also to be ready to suffer their seeming not to notice or care, and even, as sometimes happens, their discourtesy. I mention this academic work only because it seems to be what God is asking of me now. But being a slave means also being ready for more, anything more.

SMUGNESS. God so hates religious smugness and self-satisfaction and the certainty that the other is a sinner and will go to hell that he would empty hell completely of the sinners who deservedly belong there and place the smug one there all alone to pass an eternity of painful astonishment, learning that

God has mercy on whom he will. Should some faint sense of desiring to adore the One who is so merciful crack even slightly the bitterness of this so terribly misused virtuous one, maybe then even hell would be emptied of him.

In short, it is not for me to judge, not for me to presume to pronounce on others. "The last shall be first, and the first last."

SOUL. It is possible to catch sight of my soul if I watch myself closely with a certain kind of attention. Here I stand in my body, receiving in my body through the senses a huge amount of data from the world surrounding my body. It is constantly flowing through. None of that is my soul. But if I also watch myself while I am doing this, while I am receiving the data, I can sometimes catch sight of an *I* who is none of these material and sensory things, including the instrument, the body, that registers them. Instead, I see myself as an *I* that on that level is sheer subject. It is sovereign, noble, almost majestic. In any case, it exists above and beyond and throughout the body. It is an *I* so forceful in its being that its very existence is a knowing that—though joined to the body—it is destined to endure beyond it and even now not necessarily to be affected by the body's misfortunes and aging processes.

To be such an *I*, to catch a glimpse of oneself as such an *I*, is the knowledge of one's immortality.

I am not speaking here of a rational demonstration of the soul's existence and its immortality. I am describing the existential encounter with oneself and the existential knowledge that ensues. I am I. And that being so, how could I not always be?

One could object that a rhetorical question delivered like that under the force of some strong sense of self could be pure delusion. Just because I exist, why should I exist forever? Against an objection like that I would want to suggest that such a position only demonstrates that one has not yet then arrived at the level of *I* that I am speaking of. I am speaking of an experience of *I* that delivers a knowledge of self as immortal in an incontrovertible way. Obviously my body and all of the material order is not immortal; indeed, it is all painfully short-lived. And yet something that is me—my *I*—insists on its existence through the midst of all that bodily deterioration. Thus, do we distinguish body and soul.

SPIRITUAL DIRECTION. Today V. (thirty-eight years old) asked me if I would be a spiritual director for him. I asked him what he hoped for in this, and he said he wanted someone who would awaken in him all his spiritual life, the gifts given him by God, all his spiritual talents, that none be left to not develop. He said he wanted to learn to love Jesus with his whole being.

I feel, of course, unprepared to help him, but when asked, one should generally say yes. In any case, we have here an excellent description of what spiritual direction ought to be.

SPIRITUAL WARFARE. Those who enter into conflict with others do so because they do not know how to enter into spiritual combat with themselves.

STABILITY. After a period of formation and probation, monks make a vow of stability that binds them to a particular monastery for life. It is here, in these circumstances and with these brothers, that they will practice the monastic way and search for God. This means that people intend to make the monastery their permanent home. This is a choice for the primacy of God in one's life, to build in this place a monastery for the praise of his glory. The vow of stability lends a tremendous constancy and sense of permanence to the whole atmosphere. It implies buildings, places, even furnishings that represent strong traditions and are themselves permanent. Places we live and things we use whisper to us, "You are not the first to be here and use this, and you will not be the last."

STAGE. A larger stage on which to consider the Christian mysteries—as large, ultimately, as the universe. The "play" enacted is the history of our salvation, a very particular and situated story (Israel, Jesus, the Church through time); but the backdrop, sets, props and lighting are all the physical forces and things of the entire cosmos. They are indeed a part of the play; they are its setting. But then suddenly, in some brilliant and surprising move of the director that breaks all traditions hitherto established in the theater, the props and sets and lights themselves become the story. History and cosmos, one thing. Saved!

STREETS. Every city does it, some more effectively than others. Paris is especially striking for how well it is done. I mean the naming of streets. So much of the place's history, near and far, is recalled. People's names, place names, names of major events—all these become the names of streets. So I move through the city, and I am constantly reminded of all that combined to make the city what it is today. The effect is to create a sort of implicit gratitude that accompanies us as we move through the city and through the day. In part it is an acknowledgment of a past different from the present. Occasionally it is a warning or a "do not forget" that might be stretched out for miles. But Paris—or any city—is what it is today because of all these names. I walk through the air, I walk under the weather where these others once moved and had their influence. I am in the city that these others, the ones named, brought to this point, for good or ill.

So, for example, in Paris there is Rue Bonaparte, and there could not not be such a street. There is Rue St. Sulpice, and you think of the church, the seminary, the famous orators. Blvd. St. Germain des Près names the abbey destroyed during the Revolution with only the Church remaining, *près* reminds us that it was once outside the city. And Germain is another whole story. Rue Mabillon names the great monastic scholar of St. Germain. Rue des Martyrs is where we tell the story of St. Denys having his head cut off and then carrying it to the top of the street. Rue Racine—well there are streets named after hundreds of authors and musicians and other artists; and so we remember them and talk about them as we go by. Rue Odéon for the Paris theater named after the Greeks. Rue St. Benoît. This was a fun one for me, a Benedictine monk, to find, and it reminds me that on the street markers in Paris there are dates of birth and death and something like the essential description, in this case, "Abbot, founder of Monte Cassino." Rue de Bac, so called because it finishes at the river where there was once a ferry but now a bridge. Rue des Saint Pères—but which holy fathers were they thinking of, or was this a nickname for the monks of a monastery in that part of town?

STRUGGLING WITH PRAYER. It is a long time now since I have experienced clear prayer, that joyous prayer of union with God when nothing else that I would ever do with my life seems more worthwhile than this. Instead, when I try to pray I feel myself thrust back from joyful heights into the middle of ordinary life. But it seems God is doing this—though I am not sure, for were I sure, it would not be ordinary. By ordinary I do not at all mean dull. Quite the contrary. People, things, and places are all lovely to me. I have a strong intuition for them, a wanting to let them be and to be present to them. I also experience this state as somehow related to God but not in the way that prayer is, not in the way that religion is. Indeed, this "not in that way" asserts itself strongly deep within me in a way that quietly frightens me. Do I offend God? How can such a question not trouble me, for what is asserting itself from within is in effect something like a voice that says, "Now is not a time for prayer." Whose voice is that? First candidate ought to be the devil, and I consider that. But the voice insists, and it is as if I am meant to learn something from it, to risk it.

A concrete example: I had a whole Sunday to be quiet and alone. So, I thrust my intention upward to where God might be and tried to tell him that the day is a free space for him in me to use however he may wish. I turned myself over to him. What happened? An urge emerged—it seemed not a bad one—to enjoy for a while looking at the bright and clever ads in the newspaper's Friday magazine. From there I came to my sun-filled room, sipped coffee, and listened to Schubert. I thought of picking up the Gospels to do some reading, but instead I somehow felt led—am I deceived?—to read the Carlos Fuentes novel I have going. Wonderful, real, awful, awesome life comes to be seen because Fuentes posited these words, this story. But just to be sure, I decided to interrupt this reading and to go to the Blessed Sacrament chapel and try to pray. I did for a bit; it was familiar space; but I could not concentrate there or stay. It is like I am turned out from it to learn of something else instead.

People and things are especially lovely to me on days like these. Even so, I feel keenly as well the limits of it all. I feel that old classic, sad-sad-sad transitoriness. In the city a scene or a somebody strikes me in such a way as to loose a silent cry within that says "What could be more lovely than this!" And when I am sure that the answer to that is "Nothing. Nothing could be more lovely," then another awareness strikes quick on its heels: the awareness of finitude, of limits, of a firm inner knowing that, good as it is, it is not this that my heart most desires and needs.

Fine, all this. But the dilemma lies precisely here. For would this not be the moment for turning to prayer, for seeking communion with God? Yes, of course. But it is precisely from this point that I am turned back, not as if in rebuff but simply to be elsewhere, in the midst of the common things. The theologian in me wants to ask: could this somehow be a traveling of some part of the road crossed by the Eternal Son in his becoming flesh and living among us? A clever question and maybe the right one. But what if it is not?

STYLE. I learn my style by imitating. I imitate my parents, my teachers, what I find in the great texts; I learn the moves of my profession or trade. In short, style comes from recognizing my debt to tradition. But that is not the whole of it, for how I shall combine all that I receive is what makes my style unique, even if only decipherable against the backdrop of tradition. How to give to all that has already been given the freshness of a new presence, the freshness of a new me deciding? This is the drama of a life unfolding. My language already exists, but no one has used it precisely the way I will. The body has a repertoire of gestures practiced in cultures through millennia, but no one has moved quite the way I will. The wonderful tension between all that we receive and each one's originality!

S URPRISE. Fortunately, God is not what we think he is—not in any small way what I might think, nor in any big way the sum total of what a whole bunch of thinkers, great thinkers through the centuries, might think. And yet we have no choice but to try to think what God is, what and who God might be. At some point God comes to meet such thoughts. He arrives and appears as Surprise. Our efforts at thought are his foil. Shaken off of them, his mystery shines. And something new is grasped in the surprise; something is learned; experience—it could be called experience with God—is gained. But God remains infinitely free, infinitely out of our control in whatever we come to know of him.

God is a Someone. God is not a big thing that can be thought and contended with alongside the other things of this world. God is rather an infinite, sovereign, free Other-than-me who surprises by a completely unlooked-for personal coming down on me as the Force that rules the universe in ways that I, I and all others, could never imagine. I bow down before him with something like fear, fear because I feel him loving me in ways I never could have thought or imagined.

S URVIVAL. It is truly remarkable, the capacity of the self to survive, the sense that each of us so uniquely holds of being whoever it is that we are. Many consequences could be drawn from a sustained observation and meditation on this. How is it that something in us cannot concede ultimate defeat even as we are continually confronted with defeats of many kinds and continually surrounded by death to remind us of our own? What is it that even dares the thought of outlasting it all, whether we actually do or not? Where does such a thought come from? Is that a divine spark within me? Is that my soul?

S USPICION. I am passing away. From my point of view, this is a huge reality, a looming fact. And yet I must admit that I can hardly expect that it should matter much to more than some relatively few people in my immediate circle. We are all surrounded by the passing away of everything and everyone, and we can pay attention to only so much of it. On the other hand—again, from my point of view—I am also still here. And if that is remarkable, it is even more re-markable that I ever appeared at all in the first place. The sheer gratuity of this fact, its inexplicable and un-findable source, plants in me the suspicion that my passing and the passing of us all may not be the last word. Perhaps on the other side of the passing there is another world whose nature and sense are scarcely known to us.

S WINGING. Life would be dreary without all the things that swing. Votes swing, and people get elected. Music swings, and the big bands' notes are smooth. I swing, and it means I'm lively and up-to-date. But swinging's best sense has to do with physical things, that to-and-fro movement, that swaying, that oscillating tracing of some invisible curve that pulls a thing so far this way and then sends it back so far the other. When as a boy I was placed in a seat slung by ropes on a tree's branch and set to swing, swinging that way was like joining the world. I already somehow knew that the world was moving and that I was meant to move too, but I didn't know yet about rhythms, limits, momentum, gathering speed, directions and their opposites. Swinging teaches a lot of this, even if not all.

Some of the most heartrending swinging I've ever seen was when Pope John Paul II died. His corpse was being carried on a bier through the Vatican palace and into St. Peter's Square. All the while the Litany of the Saints was being sung: the names of holy men and women called out and then beseeched one by one to pray for him. Rhythm, momentum, the to-and-fro between heaven and earth. But as I say, swinging's best sense has to do with physical things; and what really made this litany and procession so remarkable was the unexpectedly slow and exactly coordinated constant swinging of the outer arm of each of four Swiss Guards who framed and walked alongside the bier. Invisible curve traced again and again, forward and back, the four corners of the earth quietly secured. Haunting, swinging rhythm that together with the holy chants was steadily, unexpectedly slowly, carrying a beloved man from one world to the next. A memory flashed of myself as a boy on a swing, and I thought surely the dead man had once enjoyed the same. Here we are in life and death, swinging.

TEACHING. In a conversation with Elliot on how he teaches Scripture to college kids, he said something that can be a concrete guide for my own teaching. If he speaks of the structure of the text, philology, etc., no one listens. But if he says, "You love her, don't you? Here's what that means . . ." then they pay attention. I must find the "You love her" in the other's life and from there begin to unfold the riches of Christian faith.

TEARS. My heart is breaking that all things are passing away. This brutal fact punctures my whole inner being, and my life leaks out in the form of tears. All that I love—beautiful earth, lovely people— all fade away and are gone. And our fading is accompanied by absurd sins expressing our desperation. For these too, especially for mine, I have tears. Yet in this anguish a hope is hidden. I find it in the Book of Revelation, in the words, "He will wipe away every tear from their eyes, and death shall be no more, neither shall there be mourning nor crying nor pain anymore, for the former things have passed away" (Rev. 21:4). The "former" things are still too much present in me, and their passing away is what is breaking my heart.

But I am writing toward my future and placing these words on the page as my own hope, as that in which I trust: *every tear wiped away and death no more.*

TELEPHONE. Aren't virtually all of my meetings with others arranged in advance by phone? Or weren't they once, and now more and more by e-mail? This may not be especially significant, but perhaps it is worth noticing. I am struck by how in London—in old novels like in Charles Dickens or Sir Arthur Conan Doyle—people would send letters arranging for a meeting. Very brief, like our e-mails, but more formal and polite. Without some means as this, it would be quite difficult to keep up contact. I think I would see much less of others. So I am grateful for these things.

TENTATIVE. I want to say something, write something, and to say and write it well. But why? And to whom? What exactly do I want to say? If I am silent till I know, I may never speak. Such silence is to be preferred to gibberish or aimless wandering, but it risks becoming deadening. There must be a way of being tentative that could be beautiful, helpful, that could move us closer to some greater grasp of things. So here is a goal for words proffered: humble speech in which the silence from which the speaker emerges and soon returns is also heard as a living, life-giving space. Silence as life, as the search, and not merely as not knowing.

TESTACCIO. "Zia" is the Italian word for "aunt." If I were Italian and had an aunt named Helen, she would be my Zia Elena. Instead the Zia Elena in my life is not a relation but a bar with this name in the part of Rome known as Testaccio, a unique and lively neighborhood. (In Italy the word "bar" is used to designate those places that can be found about every twenty paces, where in the morning you can have a coffee and a quick bite to eat, in the afternoon an ice cream or a beer.) During a number of years Zia Elena was my foot in the door of Testaccio, for it is only about two sets of twenty paces away from the back door of my Roman monastery. I often stopped in there for a cappuccino during morning study breaks as I took a brisk walk through the neighborhood. I soon became known to the owners and to the regular customers, and they were only too happy to have a monk and a priest with whom they could exchange their observations about God and the Church and the meaning of life and the different ways coffee should be prepared and why it's not fair the way they are ticketing parked cars nowadays. Sometimes I would talk with my theology students about these conversations in the bar, telling them that the insights that emerge from the refined language and paradigms of academic disquisition must still be connected with the more simply expressed concerns of the people I met at Zia Elena. I called this "Theology in Testaccio," and that became a shorthand expression in my lectures to signal that we were going to move from the level of lofty thoughts to an exposure of their existential relevance.

One scene can serve as an example of how intense theology in Testaccio could actually become. I was standing on a particular morning in a very crowded Zia Elena and was working my way over to the cash register to pay. One of my closest friends in the bar was Stefania, who collected the money, counted change back, and carried on several other conversations all at once. When she saw me that day, even while returning money to someone else, she said excitedly, "O Je! [short and friendly Roman version of my name, Jeremy] I wanted to ask you something. Yesterday I was praying the Our Father," she explained, "and I suddenly realized that I wasn't able to say the words 'forgive us as we forgive' because there's lots of people that I don't forgive and don't want to. What should I do?" she bluntly asked. The next thing I heard was someone else say, "Two coffees and two sandwiches," wanting to know how much they owed. Stefania answered, and while she took their money, I said, "Listen. This is important." I discovered in Testaccio that unless you begin your sentence in a vivid or dramatic way, you can fade out in the crush of traffic, or Stefania might easily forget what she had asked. I continued, "When Jesus was dying on the cross, he prayed for those who were putting him to death saying, 'Father, forgive them for they know not what they do.' That was perfect forgiveness," I explained. Then, not wanting to lose this first strand of my answer, I hurried ahead saying, "Jesus is praying in you when you pray the Our Father. So let his perfect forgiveness be in you. Say the prayer with him praying in you and you will learn to forgive. If you wait until you've already forgiven enough, you'll never pray it. But if you let Jesus pray it in you, you will learn from him to forgive."

There was a pause unusual for her. She dropped her various strands of conversation and stopped her shifting of the money. She shouted out over people's heads to her son at the bar who was making cappuccinos and said with wonder, "Armando, Jeremy just explained the Our Father to me and I *understood* it!" The crowd went silent, and I could see that everyone was wondering what had been said. In the little interval Armando announced generously, "Of course you understood once Je explained it." Then after that, the noise picked up again. People were still wondering what exactly I *had* said and so I repeated my short lesson, now to this group, now to that. That's generally how theology in Testaccio comes about. Lessons short but intense, and life going on all around us.

THREAD. I have this image while I pray: what God has done in Jesus hanging as a thin thread from "top to bottom" of the whole universe. It appears frail and dimensionless, without color, and virtually invisible. Still, it is there, even if surrounded all around by the vast space of Earth, by the endless space of the regions beyond. I reach out and touch this thread. That's all there is to do with it. It's not a rope you can grab on to and climb upward with. You can only touch it, feel it against your hand. But surprisingly something comes from this. I touch it, move it a little, and some new something comes into me, some new life, a new seeing. I don't go up on it. I don't follow it down, I don't go anywhere. But when I touch it, I feel a great connection.

I am touching it now. I am feeling against my hand something that by comparison with the substantial things all around me hardly exists. And yet a power comes out from this touch. It is as if—virtually unnoticed, no more than the slight movement of a thread— the door to an entirely new dimension cracks open and

I find myself standing within it. I don't know how. I am in the same place. I see all the same things around me. I am still me and I must face the day. But a bit of understanding begins to emerge and some sense to it all. As improbable as it seems, I dare to think I may now be connected with God, even in a kind of intimacy. How exactly, I can't say. I can only bear witness to this marvelous surprise. When I touch this thread, I feel a great connection. Then the connection fades. So I reach out and touch it again. Again I am connected.

T HREE. Around three concepts, I want to try to summarize a lot. *Creation ex nihilo:* from a nothing with no qualities whatsoever, God creates the universe. Before, there is only God; after, there is God and all that he created. *Sin:* a path toward a different nothingness, a nothingness with the quality of a rupture of relationship, a break with truth, moral culpability. *Redemption:* the eternal God descends to the bottommost part of this sinful nothingness and from that nothing, *ex nihilo,* recreates the world: new heavens and a new earth and a new human being.

TIME. Before time was, there was no time. Obvious enough—logically. But there was God in his complete eternity, which already included time as something that God imagined. This is not something that at some point started to be within God because God doesn't have starts within himself. In this sense, then, time has been from all eternity, and all that has happened in time has always been there. Even so, God actually starts it all one day, and it becomes something other than God, something other than eternity. Magnificent! Wondrously imaginative! And yet what has unfolded in this way from God is all destined to likewise infold back into him "so that God may be all in all."

TIME 2. Its nature, its effects, its tone, the emotions it awakens. Time is the biggest question for art, for philosophy, for religion.

TRACES. During the morning prayer today, while I was chanting the psalms, a huge desire unexpectedly passed through me that seemed not to originate from within me but from . . . the Holy Spirit perhaps? It was something to the effect of really desiring to disappear into God and of leaving no trace here. Traces are hard enough to leave in any case, but something in most of us, whether we are aware of it or not, spends a fair amount of energy trying strongly to affect the course of things, to leave traces. Fair enough. We are made like this, and it is such a constitution that makes the world go round. But what I felt this morning was a pure desire for something clearly beyond this world, for something that relativized the world and my life in it. What was striking is that the desire seemed to arise, as I say, not from within me but from beyond me. As I watched it for a while, I realized that this origin beyond me gave me good reason to hope that what I desired might possibly be had; for the One who awakened it in me was the One in whom I hope to disappear.

Unfortunately this did not last very long, and I only have an elusive sense of all that I am speaking about.

TRANSIENCE. More than once I've noted Czeslaw Milosz citing Edgar Allan Poe as saying that the melancholy of transience is the most poetic of tonalities. Yes, of course. But the dreadful pain of this thought must be faced and grappled with. And I am wondering if it is possible to conceive of salvation as grappling with precisely that. And if it doesn't, then what salvation is it? Great or small, we all pass away and are no more, and all things pass away. What real difference does it make if some are remembered with love for a while and others are discussed for a period for the merit of their thoughts or deeds? Undoubtedly it is right to remember and discuss. Indeed, it would be absurd for us, the living, not to do so since any given moment of being alive is stitched together from a combination of people and events unfolding and people and events remembered. My point is simply the absolute poignancy of it all eventually passing away. And though much of what passes is shallow and of little significance, there is also a huge amount of untold greatness and stunning, unique beauty.

So if we are saved in Christ, we must be saved somehow from this apparent passing, this apparent vanishing into nothingness. But how? Where? Naturally, I cannot offer any clear answer. Yet I sense the possibility of such a saving being contacted and "foretasted" in the act of prayer as invocation. I call out various versions of "O God, Lord of the Universe," and I am met, it seems, by a force, a power, that is going to save me, that is going to save us all. Even so, in whatever way such saving might come about, one thing is clear: the passing away is utterly real and it sweeps away sooner or later absolutely everyone and everything. This must be faced and grappled with. But I find it virtually unbearable.

TREMENDOUS. There would be such a thing as exercises for feeling my soul. I can practice and do things and live in such a way that I will feel my soul more and more, and thereby it would grow healthier, stronger, more glad. The strongest exercise is loving and letting myself be loved. What happens in this experience is a strengthening of the *I*, the sheer strong subject that I am calling here my *I*. When I love another, I am exercising myself as a free, choosing subject who, given a real choice to love or not to love, has chosen to love. In doing this I awaken to the tremendous force concealed in me. I feel and am using a power that is clearly stronger than death. In letting myself be loved by another, I feel this force coming toward me. Another desires me, and in knowing me, desires me to live forever.

It will sound like a cliché to say it, but it is still true: love between God and the soul is the strongest and most complete instance of the exercise of love that awakens the soul.

UNBEARABLE SIZES. I am asking and I am troubled in these days: Why all the universe, why all its beauty and its ageless aeons? Is it perhaps material image of divine infinity, being almost infinite but not quite, being almost eternal but not quite? The "not quite" would be the very definition of the difference between all the universe and God as its maker. I feel the tremendous tension of this difference: on the one hand, the "it was good" of Genesis; on the other, the emptiness and futility of all that is made unless it remain connected in every instant to its divine source.

In previous centuries, before the Copernican revolution and the Enlightenment busted the coordinates and expanded the proportions to virtually unbearable sizes, the Christian mind could contemplate Nature, standing in awe mostly of the Earth, not suspecting even then how much more of the Earth there was for further marveling. The planets and the stars were backdrop and ornament to the center, central Earth. In such a context it was wonderful to ponder Christ as brilliant, gracious, almighty Artificer. And though the idea seemed extravagant, it was still possible to think that all this had been created for the pleasure of human beings, as the more than sufficient context and stage for the human drama.

In my times something else intrudes on human consciousness and renders a contemplation like that extremely difficult if not impossible. I do not have to be a scientist engaged in astronomy to feel all the stars and the impossible distances between them wedging their way into my imagination and causing an old order to crumble. And since distance is also eventually time, this new length for time presses into my mind and forces a loss of all former bearings, a rhythm pulsing there that seems to say, "From so long ago, so long ago, you have no idea how long ago."

What my project wants to be, when confronted with all this internal devastation of my imaginative co-ordinates, is the creation of some new interior space, a space that can contemplate Christ as the Word through whom all this was created and is sustained, the Word become flesh and dwelling among us in these last days, a Word intimate to me and dwelling in my heart. That is a lot to hold together. I wonder if it is possible.

What would need to happen is new imaginative space. One could postulate that in our times, in this new imaginative possibility, Christ lends a new tone, causes fresh insight to what he originally revealed. This even larger immensity of the universe that stands behind the events of his incarnate, earthly life and our own—it is given and exists in this undreamt-of size as a new and more accurate measure of the sheer great-ness of God and the unfathomable wisdom contained in the divine decision to create beings capable of con-sciousness and of sharing in the divine energies.

UNDONE. I am undone by the Mystery of it all: the mystery of our human living, of our living in the monastery, of our time in the world and in the Church. Through it all the face and voice of Jesus are somehow present to me but often only as the "faith" with which I meet what appears to be his absence.

UNIQUE. Oh, the astonishing uniqueness with which God makes his approach to every soul! That there are features in common, such that we can talk about different people's stories, comparing and learning from them, is reflective of the one nature of God. But the absolute and irreducible uniqueness of each story is reflective of the distinction of persons within God—Father, Son, and Holy Spirit. The majesty and wonder of unity in distinction!

UNITED. I've been thinking and wondering how deeply, really, am I united to the rest of the human race? Then this came to me: that the deepest ground of union is not intention, even if the intention to be united or the lack thereof certainly at some point plays a critical role. Yet more basically, whether I intend it or not and whether I know it or not, I am profoundly united to the rest of my race by the nature we share and the history we share. When I consciously know this union and intend it, then it seems to me a new and more complete level of union is achieved, unleashing a powerful energy for love and for good. When my knowing and intending is in Christ and with a view toward the divine plan to recapitulate all things in him, then an immense force is unleashed, divine in its achievable proportion and strength.

In the end, for me, this intention must express itself in my monastic and priestly vocation. In virtue of my *baptism* I wish to be for my race a priest of creation and history, bringing it to the hands of Christ. As a *monk*, united to a race ever prey to lust, avarice, and pride, I wish to practice the chastity that would bend lust toward love, the poverty that breaks avarice with sharing, the obedience that uses freedom to choose God. As an ordained *priest*, I wish to let Christ work through me for the transformation of what our race creates and does into a living sacrifice of praise and thanksgiving to God the Father.

Whatever by God's grace I may do in my life in these vocations, I would wish that my contribution not be a small one but rather that it reach upward toward the nobility that God intends for us all and toward which, indeed, some progress has been made through the centuries.

UNKNOWING. I am in an impossible situation, and I feel put there by God. On the one hand, I feel the wonder: we are all of us marvelous creatures. How amazing our mind is, and our spirit, and the freedom of our inner life! How amazing the force of any individual personality! And yet we have to remember that all this is given us. We exist gratuitously through and through. And so gratitude is due the Creator. Also praise and awe. It is here that I feel the bind, for either I cannot seem to contact him or, if I do, I feel myself absurd and helpless before his majesty.

As far as such things go, it could be said that I spend a fair amount of time with God. I have the monastic round of prayer, my own work as a theologian, and a good deal of longing that I carry around with me all day, every day. It occurs to me that I have grown rather used to God, and then fast on the heels of that thought, I realize, well, then it cannot be God. There really could not be any growing used to the true and living God. Used to God! Good Lord, what a fool I must be!

Only a little reflection awakens within me a sense of God's majesty and grandeur, the impossibility that God should be and also, as a consequence, the impossibility that we should be. This is my bind. What am I to do? Surely I have somehow misconceived possible ways of relating. There is always the choice of ignoring God for a while, which God ever graciously allows us.

This approach seems to come the most naturally to us. Another approach is to enter into some sort of relation, where we at least "receive credit" for using our free will in this direction. But what sort of relation? God is not just one more thing or one more person among the world of things and persons. It doesn't seem appropriate to relate to God like that. But what other ways do we have of relating? What even can we imagine? Here there probably enters the famous way of unknowing: God is just on the other side of every way I fail to match and reach him.

Of course, we are meant to, or can choose to "confront" all this reality of God in and through Jesus. This changes everything and makes a meeting possible. But the fact that Jesus is himself God renders the whole thing vertiginous. Given that he is God, it is incredible what he has done, dying on the cross and all that. What am I to do with this? Is such love really possible? Can this really be who and what God is? If all that Christian faith holds is true, well it's just too much. I should be paying attention to this all the time. I should think only about this. Oh, I know that salvation in Christ turns us back toward the everyday, toward life in this world, but I am not in the everyday *after* having met Christ; I am in it *before* really knowing him, and I can't seem to get to him in a way that matches where he stands.

UNUSED. "Unused joy"—that's the phrase I would use to describe what Christ has done and how we respond to it. All that we need to live a heaven on earth is already here and available to us. What more can God do? With what more could he equip us? And if earth were all but heaven in this way, would that not be the final preparation for the Lord's coming again in glory? The new heavens and new earth being earth in heaven and heaven in earth.

My Lord Jesus, take me completely, and if you can find in me something useful for advancing this joy—for it is you who have given us everything and know what is useful in what to us appears paltry and meager—then use it till there is nothing left of me. If and when I am so spent, then I will have my joy in you, in who you are, in the marvels you have done on the earth.

VARIATIONS. It is striking how much one monastery differs from another and yet how quickly a visiting monk can recognize himself in the other place and easily begin to move within its rhythms. Each monastery has a genius loci, a unique spirit or genie which inhabits the place. It is that which launches the difference and develops it through all the years, through even the centuries, that the monastery is there. But when you come to a monastery from another monastery that has its own genius loci and history, then you quickly recognize that it is the same melody that sounds in both places, only here it is played in a different key, with some unexpected variations and unusual harmonies, but ultimately the same song: men searching for God and living together as best they can in love.

VOCATION. I wish Jesus risen from the dead would appear to me, just once, for only a moment of recognition, of being sure. Ah, but I know that if he did, he would give me my vocation to be a monk. So I have his gift; I have evidence of his appearance. Let it suffice.

VOICES. Centuries ago monks sang the sacred words of Scripture from huge books, three feet tall and two feet wide. The pages were of parchment and the writing in handsome calligraphy, with styles peculiar to a particular monastery or to the monasteries of a region. There were three or four monks to a book since the writing was large enough to allow them to stand at some distance and see it. What an effort these books were! Every letter of the sacred text drawn out by a devoted hand on the skin of a sheep or goat raised in the monastery's fields. Although we sing the same words today in my monastery, they are so much easier to take for granted. The paper pages from which we chant have rolled off some press by the thousands. It's easily done. We could have all the words we want in front of us. But how much harder it is, as a result, to remember that they are something precious. Each word precious, each word given us graciously by God: God giving us words that we might sing the praises of God.

I stood with my brothers in the monastic choir the other day, and our voices, as usual, rose in song. I sang from my own private book held in my own hand, sharing the page with no one. From out of nowhere and with force, this difference in books, then and now, suddenly struck me. I had not been thinking of old monasteries. I had not been thinking of anything. I was more or less paying attention to the psalms. But once the difference struck me, I straightened and stood with new attention. And as I sang, as I prayed, I counted each word a treasure, a revelation, a beauty. The words reached deeper and deeper within me until they became no longer merely human words but words God was using to say something to me. They became God's voice within me, God's message. Thoughts I could have never turned out by my own efforts, glimpses of understanding far beyond what the sum of my parts could produce—another, the Other, takes voice within me and unfolds the Mystery before me. The Word becoming words, becoming song: God taking flesh.

WAGER. Perhaps I should have learned by now not to have put so much hope in earthly things, looking for too thorough an indication of the Redemption in the here and now—people loving one another by the millions and all that, hope for history, a civilization of love. We should, of course, talk and exhort in that direction; otherwise things would be worse than they are. But such hopes are rarely realized in any developed sense.

We love our loved ones. We enjoy our life together. It lasts only so long. Then something more or less deadly intervenes. This at first glance rather cruel fact is possibly explained as a sign that we are meant for a further, better, enduring level of life beyond this life that we know. If I put my hope in such a better beyond, then I must be ready to let go, slowly or suddenly, and make the passage. If I have no such hope, then I will cling desperately to this only life I know. I will kill and fight for it. I will lie, I will steal. And even so, in the end I will lose. I will die. Foolish wager.

WALKING. The difference between walking and just sitting in a scene to stare at it is that in walking the walker re-creates the scene step by step, moving it around by moving around within it. In every moment the angle changes on what there is to see, even if what there is to see exercises the stronger force. Nonetheless, walking is a sweet exchange between place and viewer. And the viewer who walks increases in power and control over the place. The world opens more fully to the one who moves, to the one who enters it.

I am walking now with greater awareness of my control over how I will be in a scene, and this gives me peace and makes me grateful. Walking. Talking. Everyone moving. The unforgettable light when the light is right. And odd: I feel an emptiness that doesn't hurt. What might it mean? Possibly, without my trying, my center is shifting from myself to some only dim perception of God's continual and vast work of sustaining all things in being, myself among them but myself no center. God is the center and the all, the center that is everywhere. I can only let it be, consent to it. I only understand a little. I will never understand a lot. I am at peace. I accept it. I keep walking around and looking.

WASHINGTON, D.C. In mind and heart I have been deep inside the liturgy of Christ the King for several days now since we celebrated the feast, and I feel helped by the Holy Spirit to detect a little more than usual. I don't usually have an especially strong response to this feast. But this year I have that strong sense we are meant to have of being in heaven while we pray, even while we remain on earth and exactly here. That sense is quiet, clear, steady. We surround the Lamb on his throne, and the whole universe cries out to him. How odd this feels alongside where I was a week ago today, in Washington, D.C., and more specifically, on Capitol Hill. All that can be weird in the culture of America was pressing in on me together with a sense of the immense power that is wielded from the Capitol. A visit to the East Wing Gallery reminded me of how beautiful it all could be and how much America is or once was capable of. But I felt like I was visiting and moving around an empty center. The cold and the bleak gray sky only contributed to this feeling. In the airport, coming back, half the people were on cell phones having more or less the same conversations, seemingly wanting to be heard as much by their bystanders as by those they were talking to. It was vapid talk, an imitation of somebody else, a fictitious somebody seen talking that way on television. Who from those scenes could believe and understand how much more real and rich the liturgy is?

WE. It is possible to say *we* in a mistaken and dangerous way. This would be the *we* of a nation or any group that is said at the expense of the individual subject, the individual *I,* such that there are no *I*s in the *we;* their only identity is their *we.* Sometimes people are forced into such a *we,* as in totalitarian governments; other times they choose it, as in a radical and mindless belonging to a group. When there is this kind of *we,* it is possible to look at others as only a *they,* and individuals are ignored, trammeled, and even easily killed. Easy to kill ten thousand people if they are only a *they;* virtually impossible if the pain and anguish of ten thousand individuals is taken into account.

The only valid *we* is the *we* made up of real *I*s, real subjects, who know that their deepest subjectivity is engaged precisely in a relationship with others, a relationship that achieves a true and fruitful saying of *we,* indeed a saying in which each *I* knows that there is no being an *I* unless I say *we* in this way.

Of course, to say only *I* and never *we* is equally as mistaken and dangerous.

WEATHER. It is a widespread opinion that talk about the weather is always something of a nervous and banal space filler in conversations that are belabored. I have never thought this and was therefore glad to find the following in *The Journals of Thomas Merton,* entered on February 27, 1963: "Our mentioning the weather—our perfunctory observations on what kind of day it is, are perhaps not idle. Perhaps we have a deep and legitimate need to know in our entire being what the day is like, to see it and feel it, to know how the sky is gray, paler in the south, with patches of blue in the southwest, with snow on the ground, the thermometer at 18, and cold wind making your ears ache. I have a real need to know these things because I myself am part of the weather and part of the climate and part of the place, and a day in which I have not shared truly in all this is no day at all. It is certainly part of my life of prayer."

WHITE. White smoke from the chimney on the Sistine Chapel indicates to people gathered in St. Peter's Square that a new pope has been elected by the cardinals gathered in conclave. John Paul II added something new to this tradition when he decreed that, in the election that would follow his death, the huge bell on the left side of the façade of St. Peter's Basilica should be rung, proclaiming in its own way what the white smoke declares.

All of us who were gathering in the square when

the election of Benedict XVI was announced could not tell for sure if the smoke was really white. It seemed black and then gray at best. But it kept vigorously puffing away. People would shout, "It's black," then, "It's white," but it was really never white; it was just only sometimes not black. This was a unique tease, incredibly dramatic. Where do you ever get a black-and-white question posed like this? As we continued watching and trying to decide, we inevitably kept turning toward the bell to see if it would start to move. If it did, *then* we would know what color the smoke was. Finally, at first nearly imperceptibly, the mighty bell began to stir. That faintly discernible movement raised an enormous roar of excitement in the huge crowd. The bell could gather its momentum only slowly, so massive and heavy was it. So there it was swaying, swinging, but not yet sounding, gathering its drive; and it seemed our shouting was gradually lengthening the reach of its thrust. At last its deep tone sounded, and the sound propelled the movement into ever wider arcs in both directions of its sweep. Other bells swung into the song as the wide arms of the square embraced the gathering throng.

I do not mean to recount here all the details of that exciting hour. I only mean to utter a small testimony as to how beautiful at first was that swinging, silent bell.

WORDS. I'm an hour away from the beginning of Holy Thursday Mass, and I feel a quiet excitement in me about it. After this, Good Friday and then Easter. All is very plain and stark within me. Mostly I seem to get nothing, but sometimes there is a pure receptivity and something as if from heaven strikes me. Simple words or short phrases come to me as I think with excitement about the upcoming prayers and celebrations. They are the words we hear all the time, but what profound and extraordinary and moving words they are!

Love, Communion, Indwelling, Interior, Invisible, Light, Rest, Food. Bread, Drink. Earth. Life, Death, Sin, Suffering, Recovery, Dancing, Tomb, Night, Flowers, Perfume, Women, Wisdom, Wine, Seeing, Washing, Words. Love, Grave. Graceful. Gorgeous. Satan. Sin. Betrayal, Adoration, Full Moon, Jerusalem. Listening. Crying. Sweating, Cold, Love, Smiling. Touch. Lance. Covenant. Ark. Lilies. White. Love. Lamb. Family. Beauty. Relationships. Friendships. Kissing, Body, Story, Robes. White. Blood. Song. Gold. Names. Love. Sun. Interior. Deep, Hidden. Solid. Green. Embrace.

WORLD. Monasteries are traditionally located away from city centers, removed from society's central focus. Monks tend to locate out in the country and will often choose a "strong site" that can achieve, through the passage of time, a kind of symbolic force. The genius of a place is drawn out, and the whole construct and location become expression of the monastery's dedication to a way of life different from what is found in the world. This is a place on the edge of the world—but *on* the edge, not *over* it. It is not that monks do not care about the rest of the world. They care very much. But they know that there are possibilities along the edge that cannot be had at the center. They are willing to share those possibilities with any who come, but the sense of edge or margin must be maintained. Nature's remove helps this. The sense of quiet and conditions for solitude and recollection reinforce it. A dialogue or kind of dance is begun in which the partners are land, nature, buildings, the city's center, and a place removed. To approach a monastery for a visit is to join this dance. To live at a monastery is to move within this dance's moods. To leave a monastery after a visit is to return elsewhere, hopefully renewed and refreshed.

WRITING. Perhaps we write to conjure away something we fear. Or at least some of our writing has this scope. I should examine myself in this regard. There is nothing necessarily wrong in writing for this reason, but it would be wrong to fail to notice.

X-RAY OF A CHERRY. None of us can literally see the interior dimensions of things with our eyeballs, and not many would think to X-ray a cherry to see what turns up. I did not see the actual X-ray of what I am about to report, but I did see a sketch of the results. On an envelope sent from prison and covered with a number of unexpected designs, one was titled "X-ray of a cherry" and was life-size, or perhaps just a little smaller than the average cherry. Inside there could be clearly seen three children holding hands and smiling, two girls and one boy. Now we understand why a bite into a cherry can deliver so much. And aren't the interior dimensions of so many things full of similar riches?

YAWNING. I yawned in church today in a big distracted way and then felt (in a little way) guilty about it. I thought, I wouldn't act this way in the presence of someone I really cared about and respected or in the presence of someone I wanted to think well of me. So why was I being so careless in the presence of God? But then a sweeter thought followed on the heels of my low-purr guilt. It seemed like it might have been a thought directly, generously sent by God. It was this: we sometimes fall into that kind of carelessness with God because we have a half-formed thought that God is pretty used to our bodily functions anyway and, indeed, is the brilliant inventor of them. And so it can be okay to yawn more while praying than you would in a talk with lover or friend or boss. This set me free to think about the brilliant inventor of so many things. Our bodies with all their complex functions and then the whole world that surrounds them and makes them possible—all this is always underway and we are hardly aware of it at all. We're not really meant to be either, at least not all that often. It is part of the deal. God sustains us; we live a life. Every now and then we notice how utterly we rely on some vital, hidden grace to keep our bodies going; and we are astonished. This adds affection, surprise, intimate gratitude to our ongoing relationship with God. That ongoing relationship deserves much more direct attention than checking our natural bodily reactions. Direct attention—that's what I was trying to do. I found myself *yawning* while *praying*.

YOU. All my complaining about feeling God so distant from me—is this perhaps simply God's necessary refusal to allow me to treat him as an "Other"? God is not an Other. God is God. He is the *You* in whom I live and move and have my being. My whole existence is an address of response to the One who addresses me by positing me. As such God cannot be distant from me. I can only be distant from this truth, which is meant to be the foundational truth of my whole life. This distinguishes me from all other animals, from trees, rocks and all other created realities (in this realm) that exist only in passive relationship to God. All things other than the human person are created as a result of the simple *command* of God, expressing his *will* that they be. But the person is created as a result of the *call* of God. God calls a human being to respond to him, saying, *"You."* God is my *You* whether I want it or not, whether I deny it or accept it. It is as such, and only as such, that we are here. To refuse the relation is simply to be in contradiction to what we are.

YOUNG. When I was young, I was much more interested in life than I am now; but that was because I was so self-centered—not, I hope, in some grossly selfish way but simply in the way that the young spontaneously are self-centered, before they become aware of their own insignificance, when the sheer wonder of just being here is still fresh upon them.

But if I feel less interested, I do at least feel that the rather considerable interest I still have is more realistic, closer to the way that things are, to the laws that drive the universe. It is a relief to know that I am not the center of anything and not of any particular long-lasting importance. Yes, some days this is disappointing; but if this is the way that things are, I am still at least here, and that is quite an amazing experience for me. I am still interested.

ZACCHAEUS. I had gone to the new house of the Contreras family to bless it. We read the story of Zacchaeus from chapter 19 of Luke's Gospel. I explained that this Gospel exactly revealed the meaning of blessing their house. Jesus says about *their* house, "I want to stay in your house today." No matter that others might think or say, "He has gone to the house of a sinner." Jesus hears this and says, "Today salvation has come to this house." When I had finished this explanation, Alejandro (age twelve) shuddered and exclaimed, "Oh thank you for telling us this!"

ZERR. Zerr is the surname of the seventh abbot of Mount Angel, my monastery. He said it was a name of Russian-German origin. His people had immigrated to South Dakota and then to Oregon. He was proud of this and was always reading about his ancestors in Russia. Bonaventure was his first name, but during almost all of his monastic life he was called Bonny. A name like Bonny was inevitable for the kind of man he was: very large with an imposing intelligence, but totally affable and compassionate, confidant to so many of his brethren in the monastery. Even after he was elected abbot, a position which is appropriately surrounded with many signs of formal respect to express what we believe about the abbot's role—St. Benedict says that the abbot holds the place of Christ in the monastery—he was always referred to in our talk as Bonny, though in addressing him we would use the customary title, "Father Abbot."

I had already been in the monastery eight years when he was elected abbot. I had recently made my final vows and was the youngest elector in the group of monks who chose him as abbot. We are a large community, some eighty monks at that time; and to be abbot is a huge responsibility. For someone like Bonny it was a considerable burden. For he was a scholar at heart. He read widely, remembered virtually everything he had read, and was always making marvelous connections. In my first years in the monastery he had been my teacher, and there developed between us the kind of friendship sometimes possible between teacher and student. In a monastery such friendships have a special force, for they are destined to last a lifetime since both teacher and student are vowed to the same community for life.

I not only learned a lot from Bonny; we had great fun together. We had the same funny bone, and I was relieved to discover that in the monastery I would not have to rid myself of it. We used to entertain our confreres together by doing for them what we called "Bad Movies." We both had a deep appreciation for corny movies filled with failed dialogue. We would act out little portions of such films, about as much as might be watched on late night television before switching the channel. For example, an old war movie might only show this much: "The enemy, vhere are they now?" The answer, pointing at a map: "Hier, hier, und hier." The one who asked the question, expressing great frustration in the silent features of his face, would break a pencil in two and sigh. The channel would be changed. Our acting company had a motto: "He who

206

acts poorly acts twice." Not only did we have to require of ourselves acting the various roles, but we had to act them like poor actors. Not easy.

Three or four days after he was elected abbot, he called me into his office and told me that he intended to send me immediately to Rome to begin graduate studies in ancient Christian theology. I was astonished. This had not been in the cards. Of course, I was thrilled by the possibility but also not especially willing to depart immediately because I knew that his being abbot was going to be a spirited and fruitful period in our community and I wanted to be present for it. I tried to persuade him to delay my assignment for a year. Request denied.

This abbatial decision changed the course of my life. In the end, it placed me in Europe much longer than he originally intended and gave me opportunities and contacts that have definitively shaped the major part of my actual work as a monk ever since. It set me studying, researching, writing, and teaching. I am still doing this twenty-five years after Bonny first sent me to Rome. The first time I left Mount Angel to come to Europe, he said to me, "I'm going to give you one of the easier commands you will receive as a monk. You can expect more difficult ones later." After I had expressed my willingness to obey, at least to obey the command he was about to give, he said, "See Europe. I leave it to you to work out how, but while you are in

Rome, I expect you to see as much of Europe as possible." I had a sense of why he was ordering this, but I asked for a clarification of this attractive command. He said that our monastic tradition and Christian culture are rooted in Europe. The more we understand of it, the stronger our own community will be for it. In fact, Mount Angel had long sent some of its monks to Europe to be educated. I was the next in that line, and he sent another brother with me at the same time.

Eight years later Bonny would already be dead. He was forty-five years old when we elected him, and we had hoped to have him as abbot for twenty years. A cancer swept quickly through his body and took him from us at the age of fifty-three. When he was dying, I was in Rome, scheduled to come home in about a month's time. My confreres called me and told me that he would not last that long, and so I hurried home. I arrived three days before he died. I was shocked to see how much he had aged in the six months since I had last seen him. He looked very old and sick, very near death. But he was every bit still Bonny.

I sat with him for a few hours each day. Although he was weak, he wanted to talk. He was lying propped up in bed. I sat beside him. We were looking out his window onto the scene of a beautiful June day. I asked him what it felt like to be leaving all this. He smiled and quoted a psalm: "The earth is full of the goodness of the Lord." On another day he suggested we do some of our old movies again. He noted that it would be the last time. Of course my heart was breaking. But the movies were very good for us. "Philip, you never wear gloves," I said to him in a high-pitched voice. "Well, I'm wearing them for a special reason tonight, Martha," he answered. "You see, I know all about you and Duke Morgan." "Hnugh!" I gasped. Then we burst out laughing, and I knew that in this laughing we had gotten up on the topside of death, the Christian side. He was going to die today or tomorrow, but our hope in Christ would let us play like this till the end.

We switched to a cowboy movie. He was the sheriff lying wounded in the street. "Sheriff!" I shouted. "What happened?" His response was very weak: "The Kid shot me," he said. Flashback: The Kid enters the bar with a swagger and asks for a whiskey. The sheriff says to the bartender, "Hey, Wiley, since when do you serve liquor to punks?" The Kid freezes with his drink in midair and then sets it down slowly. Turning to the sheriff and ready to draw, he says slowly and deliberately and with anger, "Who are you calling a punk?" "I think you know," the sheriff responds. Then the Kid draws and lets him have it. We return now to the scene of the sheriff who had stumbled out into the street and lay there dying. Again, very weakly, he said to me, "Tell Nelly I love her." I thought to myself that he had never done this scene so well. But, time for my line: "Sheriff, don't die," I pleaded, shaking him by the shoulders. I also had never done the scene so well. Our little theater had let me exactly do and say what I was feeling in that moment. I took my confrere, my teacher, my friend, my abbot in my arms and shook him and said, "Sheriff, don't die; don't die, Sheriff; don't die."

Before he did die, Father Abbot Bonaventure Zerr was placed in a wheel chair and rolled out where he could see the whole community and address his brothers one last time. He was a great mimic and in his wheelchair made himself look much like FDR about to address the nation and hold its hopes high. To come to his very last words to us as a group, he repeated almost exactly what he had first said to us in the moments after he had been elected abbot: "In biblical times when God's people were in trouble, he would send an angel to help. He has not sent an angel this time, but I have an angel's message." Then he slammed down his fist and made a bang on the table in front of him and commanded with a loud voice, "Stop being afraid!"